The Other Davos

The Globalization of Resistance to the World Economic System

Edited by
FRANÇOIS HOUTART
FRANÇOIS POLET

Zed Books
LONDON & NEW YORK

The Other Davos: The Globalization of Resistance to the World Economic System
was first published in 2001 by
Zed Books Ltd, 7 Cynthia Street, London N1 9JF, UK and
Room 400, 175 Fifth Avenue, New York, NY 10010, USA

Distributed in the USA exclusively by Palgrave, a division of
St Martin's Press, LLC, 175 Fifth Avenue, New York, NY 10010, USA.

Cover design by Andrew Corbett
Designed and set in 9.6/11 pt Palatino and Helvetica Condensed
by Long House, Cumbria, UK
Printed and bound in the United Kingdom
by Biddles Ltd, Guildford and King's Lynn

A catalogue record for this book
is available from the British Library

ISBN   Hb 1 85649 987 1
       Pb 1 85649 988 X

Library of Congress Cataloging-in-Publication Data
Autre Davos. English
    The other Davos : the globalization of resistance to the world economic system
    / edited by François Houtart and François Polet.
        p. cm.
    Includes bibliographical references and index.
    ISBN 1-85649-987-1 (case) -- ISBN 1-85649-988-X
    1. International economic relations. 2. International economic integration. 3.
    Globalization. 4. Capitalism. 5. World Economic Forum. I. Houtart, François, 1925- II.
    Polet, François. III. Title.
    HF1411. A9813 2001
    337--dc21   00-043900

CONTENTS

ABBREVIATIONS

AC	Association de Chômeurs
ALENA	Accord de Libre-Echange Nord-Américain
APEC	Asia–Pacific Economic Cooperation Forum
APES	Association pour l'emploi, l'information et la solidarité des chômeurs et travailleurs précaires
ASEAN	Association of South-east Asian Nations
ATTAC	Association for the Taxation of Financial Transactions in the Interests of the Citizen
CACES	Conseil d'Administration des Sections Communales
CADTM	Committee for the Cancellation of Third World Debt
CGT	Confédération Générale du Travail
CIS	Commonwealth of Independent States
DAL	Droit au Logement
FAO	Food and Agriculture Organization
FENOP	National Federation of Farmers' Organizations (Burkina Faso)
FKTU	Federation of Korean Trade Unions
FSU	Fédération Syndicale Unitaire
GATT	General Agreement on Tariffs and Trade
ILO	International Labour Organization
IMF	International Monetary Fund
KCTU	Korean Central of Trade Unions
MAI	Multilateral Agreement on Investment
MST	Movement of Landless Farmworkers (Brazil)
NGO	Non-governmental organization
NAFTA	North America Free Trade Agreement
OECD	Organization for Economic Cooperation and Development
PICIS	Policy and Information Centre for International Solidarity
PP XXI	People's Power for the Twenty-first Century
SAPRIN	Structural Adjustment Participatory Review International Network
SUD	Solidaire Unitaire Démocratique
UN	United Nations
UNCED	United Nations Conference on the Environment and Development
UNCTAD	United Nations Conference on Trade and Development
UNDP	United Nations Development Programme
UNEP	United Nations Environment Programme
UNESCO	United Nations Educational, Social and Cultural Organization
UNICEF	United Nations Children's Fund
US	United States
USAID	United States Agency for International Development
WHO	World Health Organization
WTO	World Trade Organization

PREFACE
From Davos to Porto Alegre

FRANÇOIS HOUTART

The World Social Forum held in Porto Alegre in early 2001 has marked a turning point. It has affirmed the birth of a new culture, in gestation for several years, a quest for alternatives to globalized capitalism. Porto Alegre was the expression of civil society from below, not civil society from above, as seen at the World Economic Forum in Davos.

Throughout the world, there is today a great blossoming of social movements, economic initiatives and cultural reactions against social disintegration that take the form of nationalist, regionalist and religious endeavours. In short, the whole planet is witnessing a series of very varied and apparently unconnected social tremors.

This forum was a first step, a way of insisting that we know that there are alternatives to a system that privatizes the world, exhausts nature and destroys life in the name of profit for a minority. It is no longer just a matter of saying no to the imperialism of money, to the economic policies of the international financial organizations, the World Bank and the International Monetary Fund, which have become the instruments of neoliberalism. What is now at issue is the very legitimacy of a world order that reduces the greater part of humanity to the rank of useless masses and does not hesitate to provoke a veritable genocide in order to promote the accumulation and global concentration of capital.

The growing diversity of social movements is due to the constant increase in the number of the system's collective victims, extending beyond those directly integrated into a capital–labour relation. Indirect relations affect hundreds of millions of people who may not be aware of the link that binds them to the world economic system but none-theless suffer its disastrous consequences in their daily lives. In fact, the chain of cause and effect is not obvious and requires exposition and analysis to bring out the relationship between monetarism and a general loss of buying power, or between tax havens and underemployment.

Resistance grows along with the consequences of the globalization of the capitalist economy. The feminization of poverty leads to the radicalization of feminist movements. The destruction and privatization of ecological wealth encourages the creation of groups dedicated to the defence of the environment. Cultural depredations evoke defensive reactions that turn inward or look backward if they are not accompanied by adequate analysis.

This fragmentation is the result of geographic and sectoral isolation. While capital, especially finance capital, which has dominated the neoliberal phase of contemporary capitalist accumulation, reproduces itself on a global scale, resistance is still mainly local. However, there has recently been a tendency to regroup – even if this remains difficult, despite the new means of communication offered by the Internet.

As for sectoral fragmentation, it too is one of the consequences of the logic of capitalism. Indeed, one key disjunction is that between those who are directly enmeshed in a capital–labour relation and those who are only indirectly involved. The specific interests of the former appear very different, if not actually opposed to those of the latter, whereas structurally both groups are on the same side of the fence. It is of course in the interests of capital to cast the actions of organized labour as antagonistic to those who are part of the informal or black economy. Other sectors – women, indigenous peoples, small farmers and traders, ecological movements, cultural associations and so on – seem to have little to do with struggles located within the formal sector with its social relations of production. This mutual hermeticism is extremely useful to the hegemony of the market and its political expression, since it is much easier to develop piecemeal responses and repressions than to confront a coherent whole.

What is needed is a set of alternatives – from a mobilizatory utopianism aimed at a just society to medium- and short-term efforts in communications, practical economics, and political and social organization – with a view to creating a post-capitalist world. These alternatives exist and include land reform favouring peasants, mechanisms to ensure democratic control over finance capital, the redistribution of wealth through social security, and the public reappropriation of our collective inheritance, such as water, knowledge, seeds and generic medicines. Public participation at every level is key to each of these.

Alternatives, not *the* alternative. We can no longer invoke a single rigid model which *a priori* offers the solution to all problems. The transition from a capitalist organization of the economy to post-capitalism is a long-term process. The alternatives have to be developed collectively and always in terms of what we might call utopianism, in the best sense of the word. There *are* alternatives – we must hold on to this knowledge – whatever the neoliberal ideology pretends.

To confirm that human life has a greater value than that of the market, to proclaim the rights of peoples as against the rights of business, and to embrace an ethic and a spirituality which consolidates the solidarity of all human beings, North and South, is what Porto Alegre was all about. That is what more than 700 social movements from 122 different countries, represented by 4,700 delegates and more than 15,000 participants came to reaffirm.

The World Social Forum embraced dialogue with all and sundry. But such a dialogue can only exist between equal partners. There can be no dialogue between the exploited and the exploiters, between the powerful who organize the world in terms of their own interests and the impoverished millions who barely manage to survive, between Davos and Porto Alegre. The balance of forces has to be changed before negotiations, and perhaps one day a dialogue, can begin. The organizations who participated in the Forum demanded the setting up of truly democratic institutions, for in the present circumstances the very concept of dialogue can turn out to be an ideological weapon in the hands of those who hold power.

The World Social Forum of Porto Alegre allowed a wide variety of social activists to come together, from all sectors affected by the existing world order. It was an important step in the convergence of resistance struggles. What is still lacking is the emergence of another globalization, this time from below. No monolithic programme emerged, no ready-made path, but it was a gathering of popular practical initiatives which are gradually building a new balance of forces, and that means that there is still hope.

INTRODUCTION
The Era of Uncertainty

There was a time when economic decisions addressed and met the needs of social groups. This happened because participation in a community was the rule rather than the exception. But decision making driven by social needs progressively made way for a cold and blind efficiency guided by an economic system acknowledging financial gain as its essential value.

In a world where the future of humanity is obedient to the unswerving logic of capital – its clear priorities set by the principle of maximum profit in the short term – individuals and peoples find themselves subject to the demands of global economic players. On one hand the *citizen* is neglected and even exploited by a political class that has ceded large sectors of sovereignty to an increasingly unfettered and alienated market; on the other the *consumer* frets about his own well-being. Yet while harsh competition between companies, countries, towns and workers generates exclusion and insecurity for increasing numbers of people, in the North and in the South, there are also signs of an awakening of citizens and of social forces. This awakening seems to be happening on a world scale; its aim is cohesive global resistance; its values are justice, solidarity and participation.

This book aims to present an overview of this situation. Social movements, networks and analysts are given a voice here. Their perspectives chart the evolution of the economic system, the emergent social forces, and their potential for action. They formulate proposals, strategies and alternatives to the dominant system. The new dynamism finds its focus in a significant event of the recent past: the meeting of The Other Davos in January 1999. The human situation our book accosts is captured in the now famous UNDP image of a cynical global inequality: the champagne glass.

World population grouped by income level (richest to poorest)

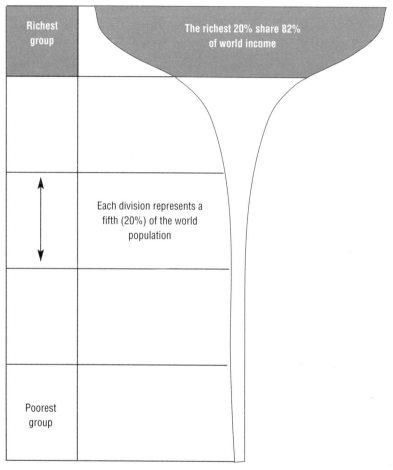

Richest group

The richest 20% share 82% of world income

Each division represents a fifth (20%) of the world population

Poorest group

The poorest 20% share 1.4% of world income

World Income Distribution

PART I

THE RECENT EVOLUTION
OF THE GLOBAL ECONOMIC SYSTEM

1

SOME KEY STATISTICS

François Polet

We believe that the main function of economic activity is to enrich the lives of all people by ensuring material well-being and dignity. This is why we consider it necessary to question the contemporary capitalist system, which offers itself for interrogation in such notions as 'neo-liberalism', 'globalization' or 'the global market'.

Statistics can give us some idea of the current state of well-being of the human community. Those collected here derive mainly from the 1996 and 1997 United Nations Development Programme (UNDP) reports. The 'champagne glass' of global social inequality (UNDP 1992) is also obvious from other income distribution data. For example,

- The United Nations notes that the 358 richest people in the world possess a fortune equivalent in value to the combined income of the poorest 45 per cent. (UNDP Report 1996)

The point here is to refuse to accept the iniquity that these figures indicate as something natural, perpetual and therefore unchangeable. They are the product of an economic system that itself generates injustice.

- Between 1970 and 1985, world GNP has certainly increased 40 per cent but the number of poor people has grown by 17 per cent. Some 200 million people have already witnessed their *per capita* income fall between 1965 and 1980. From 1980 to 1983, this was the case for more than a million individuals. (UNDP Report 1996)

- Whereas in 1960 the 20 per cent of the world population living in the richest countries had an income 30 times greater than the 20 per cent in the poorest countries, in 1995 the income of the richest 20 per cent has grown to 82 times greater. (I. Ramonet)

3

Poverty on this widening scale is more correctly characterized as pauperization. It is not simply a matter of a *state* of poverty but of a *process* continuously at work at the very heart of global economic functioning.

Looking at issues from a historical perspective, it is evident that certain people are paying dearly for recent developments of the global system.

- In the past 15–20 years more than 100 developing and transition countries have suffered disastrous failures in growth and deeper and more prolonged cuts in living standards than anything experienced in the industrial countries during the Great Depression of the 1930s. (UNDP Report 1997)

- Growth is a setback for more than a quarter of the world's population (UNDP Report 1996)

- Between 1987 and 1993 the number of people with incomes of less than $1 per day increased by almost 100 million to 1.3 billion. (UNDP Report 1997)

- In reality, in more than 100 countries, income per inhabitant is lower today than it was 15 years ago. As a result, nearly 1.6 billion individuals now live worse than at the beginning of the 1980s. (James Gustave Speth, UNDP administrator, *Le Monde*, 11 October 1996)

The developments within the world economic system signalled by these figures are no accident. They are the result of growing liberalization, privatization and deregulation, of twenty years of neo-liberalism.

The concept of poverty or pauperization might appear too general or abstract to describe a reality with many alarming dimensions such as food, health and education.

- More than 800 million human beings do not have enough to eat and around 500 million individuals suffer from chronic malnutrition. (UNDP Report 1996)

- Each year around 17 million persons die of curable infectious or parasitic diseases such as diarrhoea, malaria or tuberculosis. (UNDP Report 1996)

- Millions of children do not always have access to schools – 130 million at primary level and more than 275 million at secondary level. (UNDP Report 1996)

- According to the estimates of UN agencies, an additional $30–40 billion per year from here to the end of the decade would be required to meet basic nutrition, educational and health needs as well as providing low-cost water, sanitation, obstetric and pediatric care. Such a sum may appear considerable but it only represents a quarter of the annual military budget. (UNDP Report 1996)

- Looking only at OECD member countries in 1993, officially there were 37 million unemployed workers in 1996. This is three times as many as at the beginning of the 1970s for a total population whose growth was practically zero.

The populations of the industrialized countries also suffer from the new economic situation.

- In developing countries, growth without job creation means long working hours combined with very low pay for hundreds of millions of persons employed in low-productivity jobs in agriculture or the informal sector. (UNDP Report 1996)

The old assumption that 'the rich are found in the North and the poor in the South' is no longer completely valid: deep pockets of poverty have appeared and are spreading in the industrialized North.

- In industrial countries more than 100 million people live below the income poverty line, set at half the individual median income. (UNDP Report 1997)

- In the United States more than 47 million people have no health insurance. (UNDP Report 1997: 29)

We also know that, by dismantling large parts of the welfare state, radical reforms in the United Kingdom and the United States have eroded the important value of solidarity between rich and poor.

Scenarios for the future are even darker in terms of the social or human cost in the so-called 'transition' countries of Eastern and Central Europe. The brutally sudden change to a market economy caused their decline into poverty even before the crisis of the financial system plunged Russia into catastrophe.

- In the former Eastern European bloc, following the move to market economies, the average incidence of income poverty for the region increased sevenfold between 1988 and 1994 – from 4 per cent to 32 per cent. The number of poor people in the region increased from 14 million to more than 119 million. In 1993–4, with almost 60 million poor people, Russia alone accounted for nearly half the income-poor in Eastern Europe and the CIS [Commonwealth of Independent States, or former Soviet Union]. (UNDP Report 1997)

The problem of the indebtedness of the poor countries continues to slow any improvement in the living conditions of hundreds of millions of individuals.

- The reimbursement of debt often absorbs between a quarter and a third of public revenues, which are already limited in developing countries. It thus restricts public investment in crucial human development.

- The IMF estimates that Mozambique spends $6.20 per person on education and health. Mozambique continues to spend more on debt servicing than on health and education combined. If only half of reimbursements for debt servicing went towards health and education, it would save the lives of 300 children per day and 16 fewer women per day would die following childbirth.

When the socio-economic situation is deteriorating, it is almost always the women who make the additional efforts and sacrifices necessary for the survival of the group.

- Poverty is not lived in the same way by men and by women. Victims of a large set of social inequalities – different opportunities in terms of education, employment and property, among other things – women gobally have lower expectations than men. (UNDP Report 1997)

- Maternal mortality in developing countries – 384 per 100,000 live births – remains 12 times higher than in the countries of the OECD. (UNDP Report 1996)

Beyond the direct human cost of the current global economic regime, its unheeding pressure on the natural environment is storing up frightening consequences.

- The unrestrained and uncontrolled growth experienced by many countries is devastating forests, polluting waterways, destroying biodiversity and exhausting natural resources. (UNDP Report 1996)

- The inhabitants of the industrialized countries constitute only a fifth of the world population, but consume – per inhabitant – nearly 9 times more energy of commercial origin than inhabitants of developing countries. (UNDP Report 1996)

Conclusion
And yet – never has humanity had at its disposal so many resources and technical means for resolving the problems of survival and well-being.

<u>2</u>

A SHORT HISTORY OF NEOLIBERALISM:
Twenty Years of Elite Economics and Emerging Opportunities for Structural Change

SUSAN GEORGE

The history of neoliberalism is traced here by writer and campaigner Susan George. A Fellow of the Transnational Institute, she is the author of many books, including her compelling exposition of neoliberal thinking, *The Lugano Report*.

The Importance of Ideology

The conference organizers[1] have asked me for a brief history of neo-liberalism, which they title 'Twenty Years of Elite Economics'. I'm sorry to tell you that in order to make any sense, I have to start even further back, some fifty years ago, just after the end of the Second World War.

In 1945 or 1950, if you had seriously proposed any of the ideas and policies in today's standard neoliberal toolkit, you would have been laughed off the stage at (or at any rate sent to) the insane asylum. At least in the Western countries, at that time, everyone was a Keynesian, a social democrat or some shade of Marxist. The idea that the market should be allowed to make major social and political decisions; that the state should reduce its role in the economy; that corporations should be given total freedom; or that trade unions should be curbed and citizens given much less rather than more social protection – such ideas were utterly foreign to the spirit of the time. Even if someone actually agreed with these ideas, he or she would have hesitated to take such a position in public and would have had a hard time finding an audience.

Incredible as it may sound today, particularly to younger members of the audience, the IMF and the World Bank were seen as progressive institutions. They were sometimes called the Keynes twins because they were the brainchildren of John Maynard Keynes and Harry Dexter White, one of Franklin Roosevelt's closest advisers. When these institutions were created at Bretton Woods in 1944, their mandate was to deter future conflicts by lending for reconstruction and development and by smoothing out temporary balance of payments problems. They had no control over individual governments' economic decisions, nor did their mandate include a licence to intervene in national policy.

For the Western nations, the welfare state and the New Deal got under way in the 1930s, but their spread had been interrupted by the war. The first order of business in the post-war world was to reinstate them. The second was to get world trade moving, accomplished through the Marshall Plan which established Europe once again as the major trading partner of the US, the most powerful economy in the world. And it was at this time that the strong winds of decolonization also began to blow, whether freedom was obtained by grant as in India or through armed struggle as in Kenya, Vietnam and other nations.

On the whole, the world had signed on for an extremely progressive agenda. In 1944 the great scholar Karl Polanyi published his master-work, *The Great Transformation*, a fierce critique of nineteenth-century industrial, market-based society. Over fifty years ago Polanyi made this amazingly prophetic and modern statement: 'To allow the market mechanism to be sole director of the fate of human beings and their natural environment ... would result in the demolition of society' (p. 73). However, Polanyi was convinced that such a demolition could no longer happen in the post-war world because

> Within the nations we are witnessing a development under which the economic system ceases to lay down the law to society and the primacy of society over that system is secured. (p. 251)

Alas, Polanyi's optimism was misplaced – the whole point of neo-liberalism is that the market mechanism should be allowed to direct the fate of human beings. The economy should dictate its rules to society, not the other way around. And, just as Polanyi foresaw, this doctrine is leading us directly towards the 'demolition of society'.

So what happened? Why have we reached this point half a century after the Second World War? Or, as the organizers ask, 'Why are we having this conference right now?' The short answer is, 'Because of the series of recent financial crises, especially in Asia.' But this begs the question. The question they are really asking is, 'How did neoliberalism ever emerge from its ultra-minoritarian ghetto to become the dominant doctrine in the world today?' Why can the IMF and the Bank intervene at will, enforcing the participation of countries in the world economy on unfavourable terms? Why is the welfare state under threat in all the countries where it was established? Why is the environment on the edge of collapse and why are there so many poor people in both the rich and the poor countries at a time when there has never existed such great wealth? Those are the questions to be answered in historical perspective.

As I have argued in detail in the US quarterly journal *Dissent*, one explanation for this triumph of neoliberalism, and the economic, political, social and ecological disasters that go with it, is that neoliberals have bought and paid for their own vicious and regressive 'great transformation'. They have understood, as progressives have not, that ideas have consequences. Starting from a tiny embryo at the University of Chicago with the philosopher-economist Friedrich von Hayek and his students – Milton Friedman among them – at its nucleus, the neoliberals and their funders have created a huge international network of foundations, institutes, research centres, publications, scholars, writers and public relations hacks to develop, package and push their ideas and doctrine relentlessly.

They have built this highly efficient ideological cadre because they understand what the Italian Marxist thinker Antonio Gramsci was talking about when he developed the concept of cultural hegemony. If you can occupy people's heads, their hearts and their hands will follow. I do not have time to give you details here but, believe me, the ideological and promotional work of the right has been absolutely brilliant. They have spent hundreds of millions of dollars, but the result has been worth every penny to them because they have made neoliberalism seem as if it were the natural and normal condition of humankind. No matter how many visible disasters of all kinds the neoliberal system has created, no matter what financial crises it may engender, no matter how many losers and outcasts it may create, it is still made to seem inevitable, like an act of God, the only possible economic and social order available to us.

Let me stress how important it is to understand that this vast neoliberal experiment we are all being forced to live under has been created by people with a purpose. Once you grasp this, once you understand that neoliberalism is not a force like gravity but a totally artificial construct, you can also understand that what some people have created, other people can change. But they cannot change it without recognizing the importance of ideas. I'm all for grassroots projects, but I also warn that these will collapse if the overall ideological climate is hostile to their goals.

Once a small, unpopular sect with virtually no influence, neoliberalism has become the major world religion with its dogmatic doctrine, its priesthood, its law-giving institutions and, perhaps most important of all, its hell for heathens and sinners who dare to contest the revealed truth. Oskar Lafontaine, Germany's former Finance Minister who the *Financial Times* called an 'unreconstructed Keynesian', has just been consigned to that hell because he dared to propose higher taxes on corporations and tax cuts for less well-off families.

Changes in Great Britain and the US

Having set the ideological stage and the context, now let me fast-forward so that we are back in the twenty-year timeframe. That means 1979, the year Margaret Thatcher came to power and undertook the neoliberal revolution in Britain. The Iron Lady was herself a disciple of Friedrich von Hayek; she was a social Darwinist and had no qualms about expressing her convictions. She was well known for justifying her programme with the acronymic slogan TINA: 'There Is No Alternative'. The central value of Thatcher's doctrine and of neoliberalism itself is the notion of competition – between nations, regions, firms and, of course, between individuals. Competition is central because it separates the sheep from the goats, the men from the boys, the fit from the unfit. It is supposed to allocate all resources – whether physical, natural, human or financial – with the greatest possible efficiency.

In sharp contrast, the great Chinese philosopher Lao Tzu ended his *Tao-te Ching* with these words: 'Above all, do not compete.' The only actors in the neoliberal world who seem to have taken his advice are the most formidable actors of all, the transnational corporations. The principle of competition scarcely applies to them: they prefer to practise what we could call 'alliance capitalism'. It is no accident that, depending on the year, two-thirds to three-quarters of all the money labelled 'foreign direct investment' is not devoted to new, job-creating investment but to mergers and acquisitions which almost invariably result in job losses.

Because competition is always a virtue, its results cannot be bad. For the neoliberal, the market is so wise and so good that, like God, the Invisible Hand can bring good out of apparent evil. Thus Thatcher once said in a speech, 'It is our job to glory in inequality and see that talents and abilities are given vent and expression for the benefit of us all.' In other words, don't worry about those who might be left behind in the competitive struggle. People are unequal by nature, but this is good because the contributions of the well-born, the best-educated and the toughest will eventually benefit everyone. Nothing in particular is owed to to the weak or the poorly educated; what happens to them is their own fault, never the fault of the society. If the competitive system is 'given vent', Margaret says, society will be the better for it. Unfortunately, the history of the past twenty years teaches us that exactly the opposite is the case.

In pre-Thatcher Britain, about one person in ten was classed as living below the poverty line, not a brilliant result but honourable as nations go and a lot better than in the pre-war period. Now one person in four, and one child in three is officially poor. This is the meaning of survival of the fittest: people who cannot heat their houses in winter, who must put a coin in the meter before they can have electricity and water, who do not own a warm waterproof coat, etcetera. I am taking these examples from the 1996 report of the British Child Poverty Action Group. I will illustrate the result of the Thatcher–Major 'tax reforms' with a single example: during the 1980s, 1 per cent of taxpayers received 29 per cent of all the tax reduction benefits, such that a single person earning half the average salary found his or her taxes had gone up by 7 per cent, whereas a single person earning ten times the average salary got a reduction of 21 per cent.

Another implication of competition as the central value of neo-liberalism is that the public sector must be brutally downsized because it does not and cannot obey the basic law of competing for profits or for market share. Privatization is one of the major economic transformations of the past twenty years. The trend began in Britain and has spread throughout the world.

Let me start by asking why capitalist countries, particularly in Europe, had public services to begin with, and why many still do. In reality, nearly all public services constitute what economists call 'natural monopolies'. A natural monopoly exists when the minimum size to guarantee maximum economic efficiency is equal to the actual size of the market. In other words, a company has to be a certain size to realize economies of scale and thus provide the best possible service at the lowest possible cost to the consumer. Public services also require very large investment outlays at the beginning – like railroad tracks or power grids – which does not encourage competition, either. That is why public monopolies were the obvious optimum solution. But neoliberals define everything public as *ipso facto* 'inefficient'.

So what happens when a natural monopoly is privatized? Quite normally and naturally, the new capitalist owners tend to impose monopoly prices on the public, while richly remunerating themselves. Classical economists call this outcome 'structural market failure' because prices are higher than they ought to be and service to the consumers is not necessarily good. In order to prevent structural market failures, up to the middle of the 1980s the capitalist countries of Europe almost universally entrusted the post office, telecoms, electricity, gas, surface and underground railways, air transport – and usually other services such as water and waste disposal – to state-owned monopolies. The US is the big exception, perhaps because it is too huge geographically to favour natural monopolies.

In any event, Margaret Thatcher set out to change all that. As an added bonus, she could also use privatization to break the power of the trade unions. By destroying the public sector, where unions were strongest, she was able to weaken them drastically. Thus between 1979 and 1994 the number of jobs in the public sector in Britain was reduced from over 7 million to 5 million, a drop of 29 per cent. Virtually all the jobs eliminated were unionized jobs. Since private sector employment was stagnant during those fifteen years, the overall reduction in the number of British jobs came to 1.7 million, a drop of 7 per cent compared to 1979. To neoliberals, fewer workers is always better than more because workers impinge on shareholder value.

As for the other effects of privatization, they were predictable and predicted. The managers of the newly privatized enterprises, often exactly the same people as before, doubled or tripled their own salaries. The government used taxpayer money to wipe out debts and recapitalize firms before putting them on the market – for example, the water authority got £5 billion of debt relief plus £1.6 billion in what was termed the 'green dowry' to make the bride more attractive to prospective buyers. A lot of public relations fuss was made about how small stockholders would have a stake in these companies – and in fact nine million Britons did buy shares, though half of them invested less than £1,000 and most of them sold their share rather quickly, as soon as they could cash in on the instant profits.

From the results, one can easily see that the whole point of privatization is neither economic efficiency nor improved services to the consumer but simply to transfer wealth from the public purse – where it was at risk of redistribution to even out social inequalities – to private hands. In Britain and elsewhere, the overwhelming majority of privatized company shares are now in the hands of financial institutions and very large investors. The employees of British Telecom bought only 1 per cent of the shares; those of British Aerospace got 1.3 per cent. Prior to Thatcher's onslaught, a lot of the public sector in Britain was profitable. Consequently, in 1984, public companies contributed over £7 billion to the treasury. All that money is now going to private shareholders. Service in the privatized industries is now often disastrous – the *Financial Times* reported an invasion of rats in the Yorkshire Water system and anyone who has survived regular travel on Britain's Thames trains deserves a medal.

Exactly the same mechanisms have been at work throughout the world. In Britain, the Adam Smith Institute was the foremost intellectual partner in creating the privatization ideology. USAID and the World Bank have also used Adam Smith experts and have pushed the privatization doctrine in the South. By 1991 the Bank had already made 114 loans to speed the process, and every year its Global Development Finance report lists hundreds of privatizations carried out by various countries with Bank support.

I submit that we should stop talking about privatization and use words that tell the truth: we are talking about alienation and surrender of the product of decades of work by thousands of people to a tiny minority of large investors. This is one of the greatest hold-up robberies perpetrated against our or any previous generation.

Another structural feature of neoliberalism consists in remunerating capital to the detriment of labour and thus moving wealth from the bottom of society to the top. If you are, roughly, in the top 20 per cent of the income scale, you are likely to gain something from neo-liberalism; and the higher you are up the ladder, the more you gain. Conversely, the bottom 80 per cent all lose; and the lower they are to begin with, the more they lose proportionally.

Lest you thought I had forgotten Ronald Reagan, let me illustrate this point with the observations of Kevin Phillips, a Republican analyst and former aide to President Nixon, who in 1990 published *The Politics of Rich and Poor*. His book charted the way Reagan's neoliberal doctrine and policies had changed US income distribution between 1977 and 1988. These policies were largely elaborated by the conservative Heritage Foundation, the principal think-tank of the Reagan administration and still an important force in US politics. Over the decade of the 1980s, the top 10 per cent of US families increased their average family income by 16 per cent, the top 5 per cent increased theirs by 23 per cent, but the extremely lucky top 1 per cent of US families could thank Reagan for a 50 per cent increase. Their annual revenues went from an affluent $270,000 to a heady $405,000. As for poorer people, the bottom 80 per cent all lost something; true to the rule, the lower they were on the scale, the more they lost. The bottom 10 per cent reached the nadir. According to Phillips's figures, they lost 15 per cent of their already meagre incomes: from an already rock-bottom average of $4,113 annually, they dropped to an inhuman $3,504. In 1977, the top 1 per cent of US families had average incomes 65 times as great as those of the bottom 10 per cent. A decade later, the top 1 per cent was 115 times as well off as the bottom decile.

The US is one of the most unequal societies on earth, but virtually all countries have seen inequalities increase over the past twenty years because of neoliberal policies. UNCTAD published some damning evidence to this effect in its 1997 Trade and Development Report, based on some 2,600 separate studies of income inequality, impoverishment and the hollowing out of the middle classes. The UNCTAD team documents these trends in dozens of widely differing societies, including China, Russia and the other former socialist countries.

There is nothing mysterious about this trend towards greater inequality. Policies are specifically designed to give the already rich more disposable income, particularly through tax cuts and by pushing down wages. The theory and ideological justification for such measures is that higher incomes for the rich and higher profits will lead to more investment, better allocation of resources and therefore more jobs and welfare for everyone. In reality, as was perfectly predictable, moving money up the economic ladder has led to stock market bubbles, untold paper wealth for the few, and the kind of financial crises we shall be hearing a lot about in the course of this conference. If income is redistributed towards the bottom 80 per cent of society, it will be used for consumption and consequently benefit employment. If wealth is redistributed towards the top, where people already have most of the things they need, it will go not into the local or national economy but to international stock markets.

The South and the East

As you are all aware, the same policies have been carried out throughout the South and East under the guise of structural adjustment, which is merely another name for neoliberalism. I have used Thatcher and Reagan to illustrate the policies at the national level. At the international level, neoliberals have concentrated all their efforts on three fundamental points:

- free trade in goods and services;
- free circulation of capital;
- freedom of investment.

Over the past twenty years, the IMF has been strengthened enormously. Thanks to the debt crisis and the mechanism of conditionality, it has moved from balance of payments support to being quasi-universal dictator of so-called 'sound' economic policies – meaning, of course, neoliberal ones. The World Trade Organization (WTO) was finally installed in January 1995 after long and laborious negotiations, often rammed through parliaments which had little idea what they were ratifying. Thankfully, the most recent effort to make binding and universal neoliberal rules, the Multilateral Agreement on Investment (MAI), has failed, at least temporarily. It would have given all rights to corporations, all obligations to governments and no rights at all to citizens.

The common denominator of these institutions is their lack of transparency and democratic accountability. This is the essence of neoliberalism. It claims that the economy should dictate its rules to society, not the other way round. Democracy is an encumbrance; neoliberalism is designed for winners, not for voters – who necessarily encompass the categories of both winners and losers.

I would like to conclude by asking you to take very seriously indeed the neoliberal definition of the loser, to whom nothing in particular is owed. Anyone can be ejected from the system at any time – because of illness, age, pregnancy, perceived failure, or simply because economic circumstances and the relentless transfer of wealth from top to bottom demand it. Shareholder value is all. The *International Herald Tribune* reported on 5 January 1999 that foreign investors were 'snapping up' Thai and Korean companies and banks. Not surprisingly, these purchases were expected to result in 'heavy lay-offs'.

In other words the results of years of work by thousands of Thais and Koreans is being transferred into foreign corporate hands. Many of those who laboured to create that wealth have already been or soon will be left on the pavement. Under the principles of competition and maximising shareholder value, such behaviour is seen not as criminally unjust but as normal and indeed virtuous.

I submit that neoliberalism has changed the fundamental nature of politics. Politics used to be about who ruled whom and who got what share of the pie. Aspects of both these central questions remain, of course, but in my view the great new central question of politics is, 'Who has a right to live and who does not?' Radical exclusion is now the order of the day.

Ways towards an Alternative

I have given you rather a lot of bad news because the history of the past twenty years is so full of it. But I don't want to end on such a depressing and pessimistic note. A lot is already happening to counter these life-threatening trends and there is enormous scope for further action, which this conference is going to help define. I believe it must include an ideological offensive. It's time we set the agenda instead of letting the Masters of the Universe set it at Davos. I hope funders may also understand that they should be funding ideas as well as projects. We can't count on the neoliberals to do it, so we need to design workable and equitable international taxation systems, including a Tobin Tax on all monetary and financial market transactions and taxes on transnational corporation sales on a *pro rata* basis. We expect to deal in detail with such questions in the workshops here. The proceeds of an international tax system should go to closing the North–South gap and redistribution to all the people who have been robbed over the past twenty years.

Let me repeat what I said earlier: neoliberalism is not the natural human condition; it is not supernatural; it can be challenged and replaced because its own failures will require this. We have to be ready with replacement policies which restore power to communities and democratic states while working to institute democracy, the rule of law and fair distribution at the international level. Business and the market have their place, but this place cannot occupy the entire sphere of human existence.

Further good news is that there is plenty of money sloshing around out there and a tiny fraction, a ridiculous, infinitesimal proportion of it, would be enough to provide a decent life to every person on earth, to supply universal health and education, to clean up the environment and prevent further destruction to the planet, to close the North–South gap – at least according to the UNDP, which calls for a paltry $40 billion a year. That, frankly, is peanuts.

Finally, please remember that neoliberalism may be insatiable but it is not invulnerable. A coalition of international activists only yesterday obliged them to abandon, at least temporarily, their project to liberalize all investment through the MAI. The surprise victory of its opponents infuriated the supporters of corporate rule and demonstrates that well-organized network guerrillas can win battles. Now we have to regroup our forces and keep at them so that they cannot transfer the MAI to the WTO.

Look at it this way. We have the numbers on our side, because there are far more losers than winners in the neoliberal game. We have ideas, whereas theirs are finally coming into question because of repeated crisis. What we lack, so far, is the organization and the unity – a weakness that, in this age of advanced technology, we can overcome. The response must be as transnational as the threat. Solidarity no longer means aid, or not just aid, but finding the hidden synergies in each other's struggles so that our numerical force and the power of our ideas become overwhelming. I'm convinced this conference will contribute mightily to this goal and I thank you all for your kind attention.

Notes

1   This address was first given at the Conference on Economic Sovereignty in a Globalizing World, Bangkok, 24–26 March 1999.

3

CAPITALISM'S GLOBAL STRATEGY

SAMIR AMIN

> A second retrospective analysis is offered by Samir Amin of the World Forum for Alternatives. Amin's full text is entitled 'The Globalization of Social Struggles'. Here we present only his diagnosis of current crises, reserving his prognosis for the second part of this book.

False Deregulation

At the outset of the Davos initiative, there was significant involvement by the Mont Pélerin 'sect', followers of the 'guru' von Hayek. The sect advocated total economic liberalism with no reserves or borders, a reactionary utopia in which societies submit completely to the exclusive, unilateral logic of capital, undergoing 'adjustment' – in all its dimensions, political and social – to the sole rationale of this project. The electoral victories of Margaret Thatcher and Ronald Reagan in 1980 inaugurated the start of that programme. But after 1989–90, with the foreseeable implosion of the Soviet system, the ruling classes of the capitalist world were seized by a formidable revisionist orgy. History has finally achieved its goal, we dared to write. The socialist dream has ended, as has the dream of the independence of nations. We return, but this time on a world scale, to capitalism tried and true. The world media claimed that there were no alternatives to this: capitalism was our inevitable path. Exhausted, the Third World countries – then proposing to deepen their victory over a colonial past by modernizing and industrializing with a view to 'catching up' – had to submit to structural adjustment, and thus to the exclusive ambitions of capital expansion dominated by transnationals. Everything achieved by popular struggles over the centuries was to be abrogated. This included the welfare state in developed countries, now regarded as the regulation of a much too 'social' market. The French Revolution itself had to be

THE WORLD FORUM FOR ALTERNATIVES

The idea of a forum bringing together social movements and intellectuals to analyse world affairs and the search for alternatives was born in 1996, at the 20th anniversary of the Tricontinental Centre in Louvain-La-Neuve. The idea began to be realized in Cairo in March 1997, where a provisional executive board was constituted and a manifesto drawn up, signed by more than a thousand people across the world. In May 1998 it was decided to organize, at the beginning of 1999, a meeting and a press conference at the annual meeting of the World Economic Forum in Davos. Several organizations and individuals worked together to bring this project to fruition. The Forum plans to establish links with a series of networks of social movements, and also to set up working groups on social movements and on alternatives to the capitalist organization of the economy.

PROVISIONAL COMMITTEE

President
   Samir Amin, BP 3501, Dakar, Senegal
   Tel/Fax: 221/821 11 44. E-mail: ftm@syfed.refer.sn

Executive Secretary
   François Houtart, Ave. St Gertrude 5,
   B – 1348 Louvain-La-Neuve, Belgium
   Tel: 32/10-45 08 22. Fax: 32/10-45 31 52
   E-mail: houtart@espo.ucl.ac.be

Bulletin
   Pierre Beaudet, Rue Jeanne Mance 3680–440, H2X 2K5,
   Montreal, Quebec
   E-mail: pbeaudet@alternatives-action.org

brought into question. Davos was set up in this climate to be the high mass of the revisionists.

The real content of their programme is undeniable because at its base it guarantees maximum profit for capital, at the price of stagnation and growing inequality between the small minorities benefiting from the system and all the working classes, and between the nations of the Triad (Japan, Europe and the US) and all the rest. It is a system that fatally engenders poverty, unemployment and exclusion, often on a continental scale.

The programme therefore had to be dressed up in affirmative speeches praising the open society; the equal sign ostentatiously joined market and democracy; there were paeans to deregulation, which had come to be the synonym of liberty (without clarifying *whose*): the state was trounced as the refuge of bureaucrats, autocrats and idiots – and no longer a conceivable instrument for delivering historic social compromises, founded on democracy. All these themes found their place in a well-orchestrated campaign. We refuse to be trapped by misleading speeches that have no scientific basis and prove to be ungrounded every day.

There are no deregulated markets except those in the fantasies of 'pure' economists. Those forced to accept the markets so described will not be self-regulated but exploited. In reality markets function because they are regulated: the real question is by whom, and to whose benefit. Deregulation is the fig leaf that covers clandestine regulation (in contradiction, therefore, to the fundamental rule of democracy that demands transparency) by the dominant, oligopolistic capital interests. The MAI takes this Mafia-style regulation by the transnationals to the extreme, as the project in question gives them the freedom to be simultaneously the judges and the judged, again in contradiction to the fundamental rules of democratic law. The WTO is a bureau charged with rubber-stamping accords secretly concluded in the corridors of the Organization (in the name of the confidentiality of private business) by the oligopolies. The precarious state of wage earners is due not to deregulation, but to the unilateral regulation of the work market by the bosses. Rarely do we see accepted procedural rules so similar to those practised by the Mafia.

The neoliberal programme has been implemented simultaneously – but not coincidentally – with the development of a structural crisis of capitalism of gigantic proportions. This programme therefore becomes the way of handling this crisis. The imbalance between production capacities, on one hand, and those of consumption on the other – deepened by growing inequalities, themselves the result of neoliberal policies – engenders a surplus that cannot be invested in the expansion of productive systems. To avoid the devaluation of capital – what most billionaires fear most – they need to create alternative means to fund the system. Monetarism, floating exchanges, the foreign debt of Third World and former Eastern-bloc countries, and the American deficit together make up the means of managing this crisis. This explains the seeming paradox that the levels of profit (especially those of investments) have been increasing. Stock market values have been rising with every announcement of 'good news' – economic stagnation, dismantling of industry, the growth of unemployment. The 'success' of this policy has actually been to deepen a social catastrophe.

While the most fanatical supporters of 'deregulation' remain entrenched in the 'regulationist', there is no question of them allowing the migration of workers. Yet if such migration is regulated while the trade in goods and the transfer of capital are given free reign, the inevitable result is the aggravation of development inequalities among nations.

The Degradation of Democracy

Neoliberalism's project of economic globalization entails the degradation of democracy which, if it does not promote social progress, loses its sense and credibility. In rich and powerful countries with an established parliamentary tradition, neoliberalism reinforces a dangerous slide towards what can be called 'low-intensity democracy', a choice among illusory alternatives when – whether you vote white, green, blue or red – your fate as a citizen no longer depends on the government you have 'chosen' but on the whims of the market, on the (secret) strategies of the oligopolies, on the decisions of a central bank which is 'independent' of citizens, but not of financial markets. In other, more fragile countries, hopes placed in the virtues of a multi-party system are soon destroyed. Victories delivered to the contenders at the price of struggles often too costly in resources and human lives are precarious. There is a danger that multi-partyism, as a manipulable and repetitive farce, will become the only image that 'market democracy' offers to its people.

Under these circumstances it is not surprising that the world system produced by neoliberal politics should be founded on hegemony, arrogance, military intervention and the cynical manipulation of double standards. Neoliberalism systematically produces social crises; it faces permanent revolt and inevitable explosions. This results in continuous 'peacekeeping' requiring, among other things, a world police force. Neoliberalism demands adherence to Washington's hegemonistic strategy, and this is why – despite market conflicts between themselves and the reservations they occasionally express about cultural homo-genization, for example – the Triad countries remain in the slipstream of the United States. They are incapable of liberating themselves from the logic of neoliberal globalization, and this leaves their governments with no other role but simply encouraging the arrogance of the United States. The bombing of Iraq, a decision taken unilaterally by Washington despite reservations expressed by the UN, is the most striking proof of this so far. It is a sad observation that not since Hitler's day has a government so blatantly composed a false report to give credence to premeditated military aggression. Will the UN really suffer the fate of the League of Nations? Will it be judged a useless encumbrance, as charged in the American press in terms that sound a terrible reminder of those once wielded against the League of Nations?

Neoliberalism has not produced a 'new world order' to strengthen the security of people and peace. On the contrary, it has produced chaos and an increase in conflict.

The Meaning of Crisis

Neoliberalism's globalization project is collapsing. In the short space of a few years the absurd myth of a free market which was to resolve social problems and lay the foundations for democracy has crumbled away. Social struggle in the workplace has begun again here and there: France, Italy, Germany, Korea. The arrogant discourse of neoliberalism has been punctured. At the same time, the extension of financial globalization, in which Russia and the South-east Asian countries played a part in the second half of the 1990s, is leading to the financial bankruptcy of these same countries, contributing to the collapse of a significant part of the neoliberal system, a global financial market. These 'economic crises' have been accompanied by political crises, whether in Russia or ex-Yugoslavia, in Central Africa or the Middle East, and all have appeared to be endless and without solution – at least within the framework of globalizing political management.

The crisis in the South-east Asian countries and Korea was predictable and was foreseen by political analysts on the spot. In the 1980s these countries – and China too – were able to take advantage of the world crisis, playing a part in globalization by cashing in on their 'comparative advantage' of cheap labour, by calling for foreign investment and by signing up their development projects within a nationally governed strategy (in the case of China, Vietnam and Korea, but not the South-east Asian countries). In the 1990s Korea and South-east Asia became increasingly open to economic globalization, while China and India underwent a certain isolation in this respect. Mobile foreign capital surpluses were attracted by high economic growth in these regions; these capital flows did not contribute to increased growth, however, but rather to inflation in real-estate value and investment. A few years later the financial bubble burst, as had been predicted.

Political reactions to this crisis were interesting and new (in the sense that they were fundamentally different to those created by the crisis in Mexico, for example). The United States and its supporter, Japan, tried to take advantage of the Korean crisis by dismantling that country's manufacturing system (on the pretext that it was controlled by oligopolies) and placing it under the control of ... well, American and Japanese oligopolies. The powers in the region tried to resist this take-over by questioning their role in economic globalization (Malaysia opted to re-introduce exchange control) or, as in the case of China and India, by suppressing their participation in the process. It was this financial collapse which led the G7 to evolve a new strategy, thus opening the door to a crisis in liberal thinking.

The Russian crisis in August 1998 was not the product of a 'transposal' of the South-east Asian crisis, as has often been claimed. It was the predictable result of policies which had been implemented since 1990. These policies allowed dominant global capital interests to develop a strategy of pillaging Russian industry both directly and indirectly through local commercial and financial intermediaries (by diverting massive surpluses generated by industry to these intermediaries and to foreign capital). The destruction of the entire productive capacity of the country, with the resulting prospect of Russia's reduction to a simple exporter of petrol and mined products, fitted well with global geo-strategic aims. Quite apart from the social upheaval this caused, it prepared the ground for the potential political fragmentation of the country as a sequel to the dismemberment of the former Soviet Union. For the United States, Russia, like China and India, is 'too big' (only the US has the right to be a big country) and a threat to its world dominance.

The plunge towards crisis was accelerated when Russia entered the global financial market in 1994–6. Yet it is interesting to note that political fall-out from the crisis (the relative neutralization of Boris Yeltsin's presidential power and the choice of Evgeni Primakov as Prime Minister) may have checked the strategy of transition to capitalism, re-establishing a modicum of national control over this process.

The political crises in the Middle East, ex-Yugoslavia and Central Africa demonstrate that the political management of globalization under US direction is increasingly running into difficulties. In the Middle East the American–Israeli project to create a zone which is economically and financially integrated under the leadership of Washington and Tel Aviv has not thrived, despite the unconditional support of some autocratic regimes and the US Gulf protectorates (themselves under US military occupation). Faced with this setback, Washington opted for resolute support of Israel's expansionist plan without openly contravening the Oslo accord. Simultaneously, the US is using the situation created by the Gulf War in 1990 to legitimize its military control over the biggest oil region in the world. This means maintaining its aggressive policy towards Iraq, witness Operation Desert Fox (Operation Monica to the Arabs), which arrogantly violated all international laws.

In ex-Yugoslavia and Central Africa, the chaos created by neoliberal options continues to encourage ethnic cleansing and is unlikely to find a solution, military or otherwise, within the global neoliberal framework.

Arguments for Managing the World System

The themes advanced *ad nauseam* by the ubiquitous propaganda machines orchestrated by the dominant media corporations to legitimize this unacceptable world system have lost their credibility, whether they choose to dwell on 'democracy', 'terrorism' or 'nuclear danger'.

The accolade of democracy is conferred or refused according to neoliberal whim. Thus the Russian leaders who subscribed to the injunctions of the G7 and the IMF are 'democrats', despite their armed overthrow of Parliament, the Tsarist constitution drawn up in 1993, or their declaration that they would ignore election results.

The theme of terrorism, as everyone knows, gives rise to a boundless media flow. But rarely if ever is the role of the US government and its agencies (particularly the CIA) questioned in this respect, although, for example, it continues to fund, train, equip and give tireless support to the Taliban terrorists in Afghanistan. Even the staunchest supporters of 'women's rights' within the American establishment do not question US support of the Taliban, when the latter's record on this score is well known. There are, no doubt, other interests at stake, such as those linked to the oil fiefdoms of Central Asia. A certain Third World country accused, wrongly or rightly, of having sheltered a group of terrorists suffers severe condemnation and is subjected to a blockade which starves its people. But will this harsh light of international law, set up to judge the crimes of the highest leaders of state, ever be trained in judgement on the US, whose victims are so much more numerous than those of all the other terrorists?

When Israeli soldiers killed a woman and her six children on Lebanese territory, which they had occupied in violation of all UN resolutions, this was not called terrorism. When the Lebanese citizens took their revenge and killed an Israeli soldier, however, this was quite clearly an act of terrorism. Such examples of the cynical use of the double standard could be cited without end. The criterion which emerges most clearly is the degree to which those to be judged either refuse or submit to the requirements of neoliberal globalization and the injunctions of its empowered instruments.

The fears people entertain of exponential growth in the production of weapons of mass destruction, both nuclear and other, are quite legitimate. But global neoliberal governance tries to neutralize these fears by promoting a 'non-proliferation treaty' on nuclear weapons which imposes what some call 'nuclear apartheid': only certain countries (the five of the Security Council, but also Israel) are given the right to hold such arms. Yet the main danger, some would say, is precisely from those countries that might not hesitate to use such weapons if long-distance bombing (the kind that doesn't put 'our boys' in danger) was shown to be ineffective.

The intensification of social struggle, the disintegration of entire areas of financial globalization, and the loss of credibility of the dominant discourse have already brought crisis to the neoliberal system and its ideology. It is in the light of this crisis that we must examine the defensive strategy proposed by the G7 after the debacle in South-east Asia.

Notably, why did the G7 institutions change the terms of their discourse overnight? The term 'regulation', until then taboo, was resurrected. We must 'regulate international financial speculation', proposed Joseph Stiglitz, economist-in-chief at the World Bank, in opening a debate to define the new 'Washington consensus'. Meanwhile the arch-speculator George Soros published a study under the eloquent title *The Crisis of Global Capitalism*. We should be clear that these are elements in a common strategy which has the objective of perpetuating the dominance of transnational capital. None of the people concerned are credible. They have all been responsible for the disaster. Watching them trying to place the responsibility for the failure of their system on others affords a somewhat cynical pleasure, and that is as far as we should let it go.

We should not underestimate the danger of this about-face. Many well-intentioned people are in danger of being duped. The World Bank has already been trying, over the past few years, to engage NGOs in a discourse it presents as 'the struggle against poverty'. Faced with this apparent reformulation of the plan for liberal globalization, which does not really prioritize the welfare of ordinary people at all, we must develop our own independent proposals, which are based on social struggle and which only the victims of the present system can lead.

4

THE MECHANISMS OF EXCLUSION

CHRISTOPHE AGUITON, RICCARDO PETRELLA AND
CHARLES-ANDRÉ UDRY

We now turn to a text by Riccardo Petrella (economist at the Catholic
University of Louvain), Charles-André Udry (a Swiss economist) and
Christophe Aguiton (militant trade unionist, secretary of ATTAC). We
consider here only the first, more analytic, part of this text, which we
return to again in Part II.

The World Economic Forum has met every year for almost twenty
years at Davos, Switzerland, to rethink and reorientate the world
economy according to the interests of capital. It brings together world
powers and represents an important, albeit informal, environment in
which to discuss global economic strategy.

Davos Is No Longer Acceptable, It Lives in the Past

The priorities of the 'Men of Davos' are not those of the inhabitants of
the earth. They do not take into account the living conditions, needs,
aspirations and capabilities of some five billion human beings, but are
exclusively concerned with the interests of the social groups which,
throughout the world, own the property and, above all, control the
decision making about the allocation of the planet's material and
immaterial resources. The political, economic and social choices which
these men have made over the past thirty years have actually increased
disorder and inequality within and between countries; violence has
been an inevitable consequence.

The 'system' which they have produced – and reproduce with
tenacity – is leaking at every seam. Even among the 'Men of Davos',
voices have multiplied demanding urgent reforms right at the heart of
the system, in the current 'world financial architecture'. The fragility of
this system – undermined, among other things, by exchange rate
instability, market volatility, the development of derivatives, and the

structural deficiencies of the institutions (the IMF and the World Bank) upon which the financial system rests – is now admitted by all. The 1994 Mexican crisis and the Asian crisis since 1997 have been just the major confirmations of a systemic collapse for which the price has been paid by local populations (more than 200 million people). It is evident, therefore, that one cannot construct the future of the world by granting the priorities of the 'Men of Davos'. They represent a past which is unacceptable and intolerable.

The Crisis Has Not Just Come Out of the Blue

The crisis is indeed the end result of their choices: it has not just emerged out of the blue. A decade after the champions of globalized financial capital proclaimed the 'end of history' and the arrival of a new world order of prosperity based on 'democracy and the market', the majority of the planet's working populations have been subjected to the burden of international recession spreading out in leaps and bounds from Asia: recession and deflation in the world's second economy, Japan; recession and even depression in various East Asian countries since the first quarter of 1997; the collapse of the Russian economy in 1994 and its financial bankruptcy in July 1998; brutal recession in the leading economy of Latin America, Brazil; and the beginning of the downturn in the economies of the OECD countries.

The mechanisms of this latest international capitalist recession, which some see as the 'first crisis of world capitalism', are well known: contraction in production and trade; deflationary trends; massive growth in the volume of loans accumulated by international banks on countries or on the major industrial and banking groups, loans which become transformed into irrecoverable debts; brutal capital withdrawals from countries by the major financial operators, which live on revenue from parasitical investments in bonds, shares and derivatives. All these reveal a crisis in the system which has become prolonged and exacerbated since the start of the 1970s.

Instigators of Disorder, Inequality and Violence

Ronald Reagan's 'Star Wars' and the technological advance of the OECD countries, along with the resultant productivity differential, accelerated the crisis in a Soviet economy which had been blatantly unhealthy ever since the end of the 1960s – as was confirmed by the first debate launched by the *nomenklatura* on the urgent need for reform. The reformist efforts of Mikhail Gorbachev, emanating from within what was called the 'bureaucratic universe', rested on a fragile base. With the help of pressure from the West, they resulted in the implosion and collapse of the USSR.

The end of the Cold War is certainly not to be regretted. But during the 1990s the transition, in terms of military power, from a superpower duopoly to a world monopoly destabilized the delicate balance which had enabled the international multilateralism of the United Nations to function, well or badly, during the 1960s and 1970s (following 'defrosting' and decolonization – both the result of social, cultural, democratic and national struggles).

The Weakening of the UN

In ten years, the United Nations system has sustained a knock-out blow – ironically just when it was celebrating the fiftieth anniversaries of its creation (1995) and the Universal Declaration of Human Rights (1998). 'The UN is dead!' exclaimed the Belgian Foreign Affairs Minister on 26 December 1998, following another bombardment of Iraq by United States and British aircraft. With the possible exception of the United Nations Children's Fund (UNICEF), the humanitarian agency dependent on donations for its finances, all the global UN institutions – such as the United Nations Educational, Social and Cultural Organization (UNESCO), the Food and Agriculture Organization (FAO), the World Health Organization (WHO), the International Labour Organization (ILO), or the United Nations Conference on the Environment and Development (UNCED) – have been considerably weakened and are battling for financial survival.

The spirit of international cooperation and solidarity (in the world of linked aid) is at its lowest point (the developed countries contribute less than 0.2 per cent of their GNP, whilst in 1980 they committed themselves to at least 0.7 per cent). 'Help yourselves, heaven will help you' or 'Forget aid, compete': this is the new doctrine as preached and imposed by the leaders of the most powerful nations. Thus, the only international organizations which have any real influence on world affairs are those economic and financial organizations (the World Bank, the IMF, the WTO) where, often, decisions are influenced and even prepared by private organizations such as the International Chamber of Commerce, the Club of London (private lending banks), or the various committees dealing with norms and standards. Financially dependent on the developed countries, the World Bank, the IMF and the WTO are effectively under their political control.

The Reign of Finance

The neo-monetarist credo imposed by the United States since 1971, the complete adhesion to 'market forces' (which George Soros defined as 'market integration') and the consequent ripples, throughout the world, of liberalization, deregulation and privatization measures have devastated politics, weakened the representative democratic institutions and colonized the state. Through the choices they have made, the 'Men of Davos' have dismantled the welfare state and struck down the mixed economy, the cooperatives, the mutual societies and the social solidarity which were linked to a strong trade union presence in the United States and in Europe.

These decision makers have also overturned the enterprise structures through mergers, acquisitions and strategic alliances. The industrial and financial landscape is increasingly dominated by giant corporate networks which are outside all democratic political control (consider, for example, the case of mutual funds, pension funds or hedge funds). They have undermined economic ethics by sacrificing the objective of social well-being and full employment to the demands of the rate of profit and thus to increasing shareholder value.

They have brazenly transferred power to finance, and sovereignty to monetary policy. They have secured the independence of the central banks from politics but not from the financial markets and the tiny minorities who organize and exploit them in their own interests. They have reduced everything to the status of merchandise, including sport, art, culture, and even human beings (now signified as the liberty accorded to a patented human gene). Everything has become a resource to be exploited and made profitable. For the masters of this world, human beings have also become 'human resources'.

The Imposition of a World Culture

They claim to have been promoting the emergence of a world culture, since they succeeded in imposing the globalization of consumer markets for their products and services. In a world where priority is given to the accumulation of money and to the commercial value of 'things', they have helped to amplify and globalize the phenomenon of corruption. The liberalization of the movement of capital since 1974 has greatly facilitated the recycling of 'dirty money' – from the sale of drugs and arms through to the pickings of white-collar criminality – in legalized tax havens and, thanks to banking secrecy, through the financial and industrial organizations otherwise respected in countries 'of excellence' reputed for their professionalism and democratic institutions. In a time of predatory trade globalization, they have even succeeded in corrupting the Olympic Games and its supreme Committee.

Although they claim to be promoting cultural diversity and the joy of living together, their globalization – via world television (dominated by the likes of CNN), the Internet and global cyberspace, world tourist operators and credit card companies – has also succeeded in stirring up fear and the rejection of the other, intolerance and hatred, and conflicts which they cynically allow to be presented as the ethnic and cultural 'small wars' which will dominate the future of the world.

The Pillage of the Ecosystem and the Inequality of Income

In the midst of all this the ecosystem, Earth, is being pillaged. One paradox amongst others is that, when they talk of the integrated and desirable management of the planet, they do not mean how to avoid producing increasing amounts of waste and pollution, but how these same wastes can be managed in a profitable and privatized way. This is the source of solutions based on shares in the 'right-to-pollute market' and refined concepts such as 'underpolluted' Third World countries suitable for dumping. These 'Men of Davos' adore the objective of 'zero inflation' but they mistrust that of 'zero pollution'. The negative external effects (diseconomies, social costs) do not preoccupy them excessively. It is the cost of progress, they say: 'humanity must pay if it is to advance'. Like social injustice, social inequalities and discrimination towards women, all of which increasingly go hand in hand, the degradation of the environment has always existed, they say, and 'we' must pay the price that we must pay.

In reality, up to the mid-1970s inequalities of income between the inhabitants of the same country tended to decline – excluding those with a personal fortune or an inheritance – thanks to the redistributive effects of the state and of social welfare. Simultaneously, the rate of growth of the inequalities between countries also declined. From about 1980 inequalities between people increased sharply. According to the 1998 UNDP report, income inequality between the populations of the richest countries and those of the poorest countries has increased even more markedly since the beginning of the 1990s.

World Capitalist Archipelago: Globalization Is Not Everywhere

To speak of globalization as the 'Men of Davos' do is simply a sham. There is no real globalization of society, economy, or the human condition. There is no globalization of political regulation, of state or democratic institutions which provide guarantees and exert control over decisions affecting the various regions and populations in the general interest of the world at large.

What they have constructed, these past thirty years, is not a globalized economy, but *the world archipelago of capitalist islands* – large or small – where they have concentrated present-day global scientific and technological capacity (more than 92 per cent of world Research and Development expenditure, more than 90 per cent of patents and installed computer capacity), financial power, symbolic power and media power. This 'globalization' is taking place in the form of a growing polarization of the international economy.

Some 30 cities represent the infrastructure, the brain and the heart of this archipelago: New York, Los Angeles, Chicago, San Francisco, Detroit, Miami, Toronto, Montreal, Houston, London, Paris, Frankfurt, Munich, Stuttgart, the Ruhr, the Dutch Ranstad, Copenhagen, Milan, Rome, Madrid, Barcelona, Stockholm, Tokyo, Osaka, Nagoya, Shanghai, São Paulo, Hong Kong, Singapore.... In these cities lie the major business centres of the world, the hearts of the communication and information networks and the headquarters of the largest industrial, financial and commercial multinationals. Liberalization, deregulation, privatization and competition have ensured that the links between them draw ever tighter than the links from them to the rest of the world. The famous 'world village' is just an archipelago.

The 'Men of Davos' say that the innovations which count are generated in and produced by these islands, certain of which (such as Silicon Valley) have been elevated to the level of paradigms to be universalized. According to them, these islands are the point of origin of the 'new information society' and are in the process of engendering the 'knowledge society', the universe of dematerialized wealth and new knowledge. The only realistic option for other regions of the world will be to try to attach themselves, at any cost, to one of the islands of the archipelago in the hope of becoming an integral part of it. Those that do not succeed will, according to Davos, inevitably be cast adrift; they will not even be peripheral any more but 'without a future'.

Internet literacy becomes a necessary step for the establishment of channels and bridges with the archipelago. For this reason, the construction of cyberspace pipelines and networks is becoming one of the major priorities everywhere, even more important than the installation of taps with drinking water, which are vitally needed by two billion people even today.

Clearly, current 'globalization' has expropriated life, and the right to basic living.

Expropriation of the Future of the World

Expropriation phenomena have multiplied and been amplified every-where.

- *The human being* has been expropriated of his basic rights: as a 'human resource', he/she only has the right to exist as a function of profitability and of what is now known as 'employability', a concept which has replaced that of the 'right to work'.

- *Society* has been expropriated of its raison d'être as a system for organizing and promoting inter-personal and inter-institutional links, with their corresponding interactions and transactions. It has been replaced by the market, elevated to the rank of a 'system' that ensures the optimal form and procedure for all transactions between individuals.

- *Work* has been expropriated in its role as a creator of value and history: as a 'good' competing with other goods on the global market, its cost must fall continuously, and the leverage of globalized unemployment will be used to achieve this.

- *Social life* has been expropriated of its functions of identity and solidarity: value is given only to individualism, to the logic of survival and the application of force in a context of warlike competition.

- *Politics* has been expropriated of its fundamental power to regulate, represent and control while being a democratic legitimizing force: this role – stripped of democratic legitimacy – has been handed over to finance and to technocracy.

- *Culture* has been expropriated of its variety, drama and sublimity: in its place has been put technology, numbing standardization, the violence of instincts and the barbarism of force.

- *The town* has been expropriated of its function as a community area: it has been turned into a place of non-belonging, flux and speed, a place where one fits or one is lost in a permanent nomadic state without memory;

- *Democracy* has been expropriated of its values of liberty, equality and solidarity: effective power has been given to a new world oligar-chical class whose characteristic traits, values and methods of operation we are now starting to get a glimpse of.

5

THE BROKEN ENGINES OF GROWTH

FRANÇOIS CHESNAIS AND DOMINIQUE PLIHON

> Whilst the preceding text highlights the sovereignty deficit resulting from globalization, the contribution from ATTAC looks at new financial forms of global capitalism. It is written by Dominique Plihon and François Chesnais, economists and members of ATTAC's Scientific Council.

Since financial globalization became a feature of the world economy, crises have followed at an accelerating rhythm: the 1987 stock market crash, European currency crises in 1992–3, the Mexican crisis of 1994, the crisis in the emerging countries of Asia in 1997, and that in Russia in 1998.

The current crisis is undoubtedly the most serious on account of its scale and the number of countries affected. It started in South-east Asia in 1997, then destabilized Japan, then in a more generalized form affected other emerging countries in Europe (Russia) and soon in Latin America (Brazil). There is no longer any doubt that it will profoundly affect the world economy, starting with the United States and the countries of the European Union. It is therefore a global systemic crisis: it cannot be reduced to a mere financial accident but affects the underlying engines of world economic growth.

Point of Departure: the Financial Crisis of the Asian 'Dragons'

These countries, which had seen exceptional growth rates, used to be presented by the defenders of the liberal order as development models which demonstrated the benefits of the globalization of the world economy. By opening up to the outside world, they benefited from the arrival of capital from the industrialized countries. Their growth was accelerated by a rapid increase in exports to industrialized countries, with whom they competed successfully thanks to low labour costs.

This 'virtuous' model imploded for three main reasons. First, the

---

The Association for Taxation of Financial Transactions in the Interests of the Citizen (ATTAC)

ATTAC was founded in France on 3 June 1998 on the initiative of *Le Monde Diplomatique*. To guarantee its long-term existence, it was constituted around a group of founders which included publications, associations and trade unions as well as various well-known personalities. It was then reorganized to accommodate individual members as well as new trade unions, associations, publications, enterprises and local collectives. By May 1999 ATTAC had some 9,000 members and more than 100 local committees.

The central objective of ATTAC is to produce information – from books to tracts – to counter all aspects of domination by the financial world of political, economic, social and cultural life. The association organizes meetings on a local, national and international level, takes part in public debates and lobbies decision makers at all levels.

ATTAC's principal focus areas at the moment are: the different forms of taxation of financial transactions, in particular the Tobin tax on currency speculation; the creation of new instruments for the regulation and control of finance at the national, European and international levels; the battle against tax havens and financial crime; and the demystification of pension funds.

ATTAC pursues these campaigns at the international level through the contacts it maintains with many groups and networks working towards the same goals. ATTAC associations have been created in Italy, Belgium, Switzerland, Brazil and Quebec.

Address:
9 bis, rue de Valence, 75005 Paris
Tel: 33/1/43.36.30.54 – Fax: 33/1/43.36.26.26
E-mail: attac@attac.org – Internet: http://Attac.org

---

growth capacity of the specialized sectors of the emerging countries was exhausted, which manifested itself in the overproduction of low-value-added goods by these countries (textiles and electronics in particular). Second, their exchange rates, which were anchored to the dollar, became overvalued following the rise of the US currency in 1996–7. As a result these countries lost their competitivity, which affected their exports, and they became the targets of speculative attacks since their exchange rates no longer appeared credible. A third factor was the shortcomings of the emerging banking and financial system. The banks were the beneficiaries of the massive influx of international capital, and lent money indiscriminately, creating a speculative bubble, particularly in the real-estate sector and on the stock markets. Such poor risk management was aggravated by the deficiencies of the supervisory authorities which were in most cases incompetent and corrupt.

Why Is This Crisis More Serious than Preceding Ones?

The current crisis is a direct consequence of the globalization process. This last, which has become widespread over the past ten years, has led to two principal changes in the world economy. The first is that the markets have become the dominant mode of regulation, which means that political bodies have lost their importance to private operators (international investors and multinational enterprises). Second, countries involved in this new order are largely open to the world economy, which has reinforced the interdependence of national economies.

The crises preceding globalization were contained because public authorities still played an important role. Thus the debt crisis at the beginning of the 1980s was a crisis involving the sovereign debt of developing countries. For this reason the debtors were limited to a small number of borrowers and in this context it was possible to control the crisis by concerted action between states. Today, the situation is totally different as the financial crisis involves essentially private players (banks, investors, enterprises) and results from complex interactions between a multitude of players obeying a micro-economic logic. This new complexity of economic crises explains why they can no longer be controlled easily.

The seriousness of the current crisis is exacerbated by the strong interdependence of national economies, the second characteristic of globalization. This explains why the crisis has spread since 1997, beginning in the emerging countries of Asia: after they had been hit one after the other in a domino effect, their ailment was 'transmitted' to the rest of the world (Japan, then the United States, more recently Europe, Russia and the European Union).

Another factor which has helped amplify the crisis is the role played by speculators. International investors play the markets to realize added value, and in this way take part in the creation of financial bubbles. But when they lose confidence, they withdraw with brutal suddenness from local financial centres, thus contributing to local crises. These movements are even more destructive because speculators tend to act like sheep: they all react simultaneously, and they all head out in the same direction.

To sum up: the current crisis, all the effects of which have yet to be felt, illustrates the inability of the globalized market economy to self-regulate. This is a rude blow to the dangerous optimism promoted by liberal ideology, according to which the famous 'invisible hand' is there to ensure that markets lead to a harmonious economic order from which everyone will benefit.

Our analysis shows that it is necessary to propose, right now, another way of regulating the world economy. We must try to reduce the two negative dimensions of financial globalization. We need to limit the exorbitant power of the markets by giving importance back to public regulation. We must, in particular, re-regulate and impose a tax on financial operations in order to discourage pure speculation. We also have to reduce the negative effects of the interdependence of economies. It is neither possible nor desirable to question the development of international exchange, but it *is* necessary, by contrast, to bring about international cooperation to control the international operators and to penalize practices which are contrary to national interests, particularly those of developing countries. Clearly, the international bodies today, and the IMF in particular, are incapable of playing this role correctly.

Such measures would be insufficient, however, to attack the basis of the current crisis, which is the deep-rooted malfunctioning of world capitalism, as is explained below.

Overproduction as a Crisis in the Regime of Financial Accumulation

This crisis is not restricted to the financial sphere, and so cannot be dealt with at this level alone. We need to look at the root cause of these financial convulsions. They herald the re-emergence of the classical crisis of generalized overproduction, the basis of which, as Marx showed better than anyone, is to be found at the level of production relationships which are at the same time the relationships of the distribution of wealth.

What is new, however, is that the return of this increasingly intractable economic crisis is happening in explosive circumstances. There is, first, a globalization of capital based on liberalization and deregulation – that is, the widespread dismantling of the governmental mechanisms which were previously in a position to manage anti-cyclical policies. Moreover, there is a certain blindness and unpreparedness among the dominant capitalist classes, intoxicated by the 'victory over communism' and committed to a neoliberal utopia about the self-regulating and omniscient nature of the market mechanism.

The crisis is thus one of overproduction within a new regime of globalized accumulation of financial capital. It expresses the impossibility of ensuring a sufficient quantity of capital at the completion of the cycle of production and marketing, of creation and realization of value and of added value, due to the endemic insufficiency of effective world demand.

Marx had a good grasp of the paradox of overproduction: underlining its relative nature, he said that, far from displaying a surplus of wealth, it was the sign of a system reaching fundamental limits of accumulation set by its inbuilt distribution mechanisms. Earlier in this century, Keynes tried to provide a response without abandoning private ownership of the means of production and with the aid of his precious 'twins', the World Bank and the IMF. But over the last twenty years the countries of the Third World have seen the re-emergence of the worst scourges of malnutrition and famine, of sickness and pandemic disease; the OECD countries have seen a rise in the number of people without secure employment, homes and rights. These scourges are not 'natural'. They affect populations who are marginalized and excluded from satisfying their basic needs, and thus from the basis of civilization – given their incapacity to transform these pressing needs into effective, money-backed demands.

This exclusion is thus of an economic nature. In certain cases it is recent and in all countries it has worsened seriously compared to the situation in the 1970s. It is the direct product of a system of accumulation born of deregulation, liberalization and the destruction not only of jobs but of entire systems of social production. This system submits technical progress to the narrowest indicators of profit by encouraging the total freedom of movement of capital to fuel competitive jousting between forms of social production with different and contradictory objectives: maximizing profit, on one hand, and, on the other, ensuring the conditions of social reproduction of communities (farmers, fisher people, craftworkers …).

It seemed a good idea to celebrate the 'victory of the consumer over the producer' as well as 'revenge on the lenders'. They forgot that the 'producers' – the wage earners – are also consumers and that, as workers in the advanced capitalist countries are sacked and the livelihoods of peasants in Third World countries are lost through liberalization, the consumer loop closes up.

Consumption by the shareholder groups who live completely or partially from financial revenues – interest from bonds or dividends from shares – can support demand and economic activity in the United

States and other 'shareholder countries', the source countries for massive capital investments. This development has been the subject of several theoreticians of imperialism, many of whose analyses, in turn, became whole new realities. But at the macro-economic level of the world system, no stockholder–consumer can ever compensate for the markets which are being destroyed by massive unemployment or the absolute impoverishment imposed on communities which previously could ensure their reproduction and exercise a certain level of effective demand.

The world economy is facing the brutal return of the reality principle: before being able to appropriate value and added value, these have to be created on a sufficient scale. This supposes that the cycle of capital has been achieved and production commercialized. The managers of the large investment funds – mutual funds or private Anglo-Saxon pension funds – together with the other major operators in the financial markets have developed yield norms for their investments. They have imposed these on companies as well as on those financial markets which are reliant on the system and which are the links in the global process of the centralization of wealth towards the shareholder countries.

In their eyes, these standards, these constant pressures, are the conditions for the flow of revenue transfer towards the financial markets at a pace and on a scale necessary to satisfy this international shareholder economy. It is beautiful; it appears to function. But, in fact, it only works provided the return on the capital which is creating value and added value – the base of distribution and the transfer of wealth towards the creditors of production – has been achieved on a grand enough scale, and without shocks or interruptions in the flow of wealth.

The financial markets which have resulted from liberalization, deregulation and financial globalization have their own timeframe which is not that of the value-creating process and still less that of production itself – with slowdowns or, worse, interruptions in the course of the cycle. It seems that the operators have no memory of past crises. It is as if they do not know, even in a vague or bookish way, what happened in 1929 and in the 1930s, and thus find themselves totally defenceless. That their response is typically one of 'helplessness' or even panic only serves to accelerate the crisis at key moments, by strengthening the subjective dimension of the headlong rush and propelling it even more rapidly forward.

6

THE NEW DEBT CRISIS

ERIC TOUSSAINT

As we will see below, the all-powerful multilateral institutions are not concerned about the satisfaction of human and social needs. Keeping poor countries in extreme poverty and using their indebtedness as a means of blackmail is an out-an-out denial of human rights. The text edited by Eric Toussaint for CADTM permits us to see the situation in indebted countries more clearly.

Since 1997/8 the Third World, which accounts for 80 per cent of the world's population, has been confronted with a new debt crisis which only a fortunate few of these countries have been able to avoid. The immediate causes of this are as follows:

1 an increase in interest rates (whilst interest rates are falling in the North, they have increased in the countries of the periphery);

2 a reduction in the flow of fresh capital;

3 a sharp fall in their export income (caused by the fall in price of most of the products exported by the countries of the South).

The Incidence of Debt in the South

The growth in the debt burden has been very rapid in Asia and in Latin America. The amounts to be reimbursed over the short term have increased, whilst new loans have been rare and export revenues are falling. Africa is, relatively speaking, less harshly affected by this changing situation: loans and investment by private financial institutions from the North have been almost insignificant since 1980. They can hardly decrease further (except for the Republic of South Africa and Nigeria, which receive almost 70 per cent of investment). Africa nevertheless continues to endure a poverty crisis with dramatic human

THE COMMITTEE FOR THE CANCELLATION OF THIRD WORLD DEBT
(CADTM)

Created in 1990, CADTM is an international network based in Brussels working for radical alternatives to different forms of oppression wherever they take place in the world. CADTM's main focus is Third World debt and the structural adjustment which is its consequence. The system of debt constitutes one of the fundamental mechanisms through which the dictates of the G7, the multinationals, and the World Bank/IMF/WTO trio are implemented. CADTM calls for the cancellation of Third World debt and the abandonment of the structural adjustment policies imposed on the countries of the periphery. The realization of these demands constitutes an insufficient but necessary condition for breaking the chains of oppression that bind these countries. Other priority demands supported by CADTM are: the expropriation of the wealth kept in the North by the rich of the South in order to return it to the people of the Third World; wealth tax; tax on financial transactions; rejection of the MAI and its clones; the right of countries of the periphery to protectionism.

In addition to these concrete demands CADTM calls for the emancipation of women; radical agricultural reform; a general reduction in working hours; disarmament; the rejection of all forms of racism; and the planned transfer of wealth from the countries of the North to the countries of the South to compensate for the pillage to which these peoples have been and still are subjected.

CADTM is active in Europe, Africa and Latin America. Recently, collaborative relationships have been established with new popular movements in Asia. CADTM is a network for planning, sensitizing and mobilizing. Its members are individuals and movements. For CADTM, lobbying action is incidental. CADTM actively participates in the development of ATTAC.

Address:
Rue Plantin 29
B-1070 Brussels
Tel: 32/2/527.59.90 – Fax: 32/2/522.62.27
E-mail: cadtm@skynet.be *Website:* http://users.skynet.be/cadtm

aspects that are even more sharply accentuated than in Asia and in Latin America.

New loans to Third World countries by private financiers have been rare since the crisis which began in South-east Asia in 1997 rebounded on Eastern Europe and Latin America in 1998. The Third World countries which still had access to international financial markets, and could issue public bonds in London or New York, had to increase the yield payments they guaranteed to purchasers of their bonds. The loan raised by Argentina in October 1998 in the financial centres of the North guaranteed an interest rate of 15 per cent, or two and a half times that offered at the time by public bodies in the North for their new loans. Nevertheless, private lenders in the North and South prefer to buy the public bonds of Northern states rather than those of the South (or East).

In short, as during the previous debt crisis at the beginning of the 1980s, credit became scarce and more expensive for the Third World. Foreign direct investment, aimed at South-east Asia (including China) and towards the principal economies of Latin America (it would cost them a significant privatization programme) rose between 1993 and 1997. After 1998, they experienced a tailing off which risked continuing into 1999 (foreign direct investment in South-east Asia fell by over 30 per cent in 1998 compared to 1997, and loans fell by 14 per cent in the first semester of 1998).

IMF Action

The measures imposed by the IMF on the economies and populations of the countries of the periphery have resulted in recession, a loss of the fundamental elements of national sovereignty, and a dramatic fall in standards of living. In certain countries, they have aggravated a situation which was already unbearable for a large section of the population. The contrast between the growth of returns to the national owners of capital and the drastic fall in the incomes of most households reached historic proportions towards the end of the twentieth century. In September–October 1998, the holders of the Brazilian domestic debt were rewarded with an almost 50 per cent interest rate, while the rate of inflation did not exceed 3 per cent. Brazilian capitalists and transnational firms, particularly those based in Brazil, could borrow dollars at 6 per cent on Wall Street and lend them within Brazil at rates varying between 20 and 49.75 per cent. At the same time, they hedged a large proportion of their capital from changes in Brazil's economic situation by taking it out of the country *en masse*.

Some Figures

Total Third World debt (excluding the countries of Eastern Europe) stood at around $1,950 billion in 1997. The Third World reimburses more than $200 billion each year. Total public development aid (including loans repayable at below market rates) has not exceeded $45 billion in recent years. Sub-Saharan Africa spends four times as much in reimbursing this debt as it does in total on health and education. Other figures from 1998 show that the debt of households in the United States stood at $5,500 billion (UNDP 1998). The public debt of the United States exceeded $5,500 billion. The public debt of the 15 members of the European Union exceeded $5,500 billion. Every year, military expenditure in the world amounts to $780 billion (UNDP 1998: 41), that of advertising to $1,000 billion (UNDP 1998: 70). Each day, more than $2,000 billion is traded on the currency exchange markets and more than 90 per cent of this amount is traded in speculative operations.

PART II

THE IMPORTANCE OF A GLOBAL POLITICAL RESPONSE

The account of capitalism's crisis offered in Part I makes it clear that a deep-going reorientation is necessary. To introduce criteria of solidarity and social justice indispensable if the world is to 'live together' in a more equitable and viable way, we must address existing power relationships. The current economic system functions according to its own laws; it has emancipated itself from the values and norms of the vast majority of humanity. Returning the human being and social needs to the centre of the economic game can be accomplished only by taking on the current politico-economic structures. It is by bringing together and coordinating different social forces across the world that we can break the prevalent neoliberal consensus and propose alternatives for a more humane global society. The present era of crisis and uncertainty can trigger awareness of the obsolescence of today's dominant economic principles.

All of the texts which follow evaluate the different dimensions of a coherent response at the global level based on constructive alternatives.

7

A STRATEGY APPROPRIATE TO NEW TIMES

CHRISTOPHE AGUITON

In Part I each contribution looked at the recent development of world capitalism from a particular angle. In Part II our contributors propose some solutions to the problems of social justice and equity raised earlier. And they ask how a globally organized resistance could motivate and activate commitment to a different world system. The first chapter is by ATTAC's Christophe Aguiton. The current epoch, he believes, is favourable for a 'counter-offensive'.

The idea of an alternative Davos has an intrinsic interest: it shows that there is opposition, that other voices exist outside the liberal temple, and that many of them are talking realistically about resistance. If it does not develop a more global programme, however, this opposition will be shown to have clear limits. The ideological climate is beginning to change and it is possible to make ourselves heard, at least, and even to claim the first victories – perhaps making a MAI into a might-have-been, although this victory has yet to be confirmed. But now we need to begin outlining a more global programme of international action.

1 Our departure point is the structural, economic and financial crisis, with all the practical and ideological consequences which we can draw from it for our action programme. We must first address the ideological changes. Over nearly 20 years, neoliberalism has been comfortably ahead on points, but now the wind is changing, and it is our responsibility to make this change as visible as possible and to make it the focal point of a counter-offensive. The counter-offensive must be developed on practical and concrete issues (MAI, etc.), and also on the larger field of social alternatives to the disaster of neo-conservative counter-reforms.

2 This medium- and long-term project is twofold. First, to support and facilitate the development of concrete campaigns with limited objectives. Starting from simple, focused and accessible issues

45

guarantees campaigns that have mass appeal, as was demonstrated by both the campaign against the MAI and the launch of ATTAC. After MAI (a campaign that continues with the shift to the WTO, where there is a project to coopt, within the framework of the American lobbying system, a segment of our opposition) the attack could be focused on the tax on capital (the Tobin tax and other initiatives), the struggle against the plans of the IMF, and the campaign for cancellation of Third World debt.

Then, we must promote social alternatives to neoliberalism. This objective is much more difficult to realize because the debates between the militants opposed to liberalism have only just begun. During the first meetings of ATTAC, as well as clearly anti-capitalist positions there were those whose priority was the regulation of financial markets and of the world economic system. Agreement was eventually reached (but that will not settle everything!) on the necessity for 'empowering the citizen faced with the dictatorship of the market'.

3 A truly international convergence seems possible on such objectives because social forces espousing a radical critique of liberalism have developed (the Movement of Landless Farmworkers in Brazil, KCTU in Korea, European marches, etc.) and because international and regional demonstrations (above all in Europe, America and Asia) are growing in strength.

To achieve such convergence, we have to take into account the plurality of the preoccupations in the different countries, making sure that the initiatives do not compete with each other and building large alliances, with numerous networks and movements developing around related themes. All of this calls for patient, methodical consolidation so that the different initiatives being proposed in various countries work towards a common goal within a joint perspective.

8

Alternatives to the Neoliberal Model

François Houtart

For some time now various social movements have offered not only critiques but also alternatives to the dominant model of society, which is consumerist, individualistic, socially unjust and, above all, cynical. François Houtart (sociologist, director of the Tricontinental Centre and executive secretary of the World Forum for Alternatives) recommends the study of these alternatives. He took as a starting point contributions to the journal *Alternatives Sud* during its first three years of existence.

A student of Adam Smith, the Swiss Count Sigmund Sismondi, visited England three times between 1818 and 1826. In 1826 he wrote on the subject of liberal economic theories: 'Their theories as they are practised have contributed to the growth of material wealth, but have diminished overall satisfaction for the individual ... they tend to render the rich richer and the poor poorer, more dependent and more miserable.'

If, more than 170 years later, we are still making the same point, both in the Third World and in my own society, this is no doubt because similar situations still exist to a certain extent; more especially, it can be put down to the fact that the same economic logic dominates society. This is why the search for alternatives, while certainly specific to the time in which we live, retains a sense of continuity with the experiences of the past. In short, we must seek a new language and new techniques to address the new forms of an old problem.

Alternatives to Capitalism

If neoliberalism is only one phase of capitalist development, what we are talking about is alternatives (rather than minor changes) to capitalism; it is alternatives to real capitalism, not simply to liberal, neoliberal or even neoclassical economic theories; nor is it alternatives to 'savage' or 'civilized', 'American' or 'Western European' capitalism that we seek.

In any discussion of alternatives, the obvious first stop is the notion of real socialism, which, after 1917, became the antithesis of capitalism. The defeat of real socialism must clearly be analysed from all angles. It is a lesson in the strength of capitalism as a global system, which used all the political and military means at its disposal to bring about the downfall of socialism. It is also a lesson about an alternative construct that defined valid social objectives and gained appreciable results, but also succumbed to its own internal inflexibility and fell a victim to its own mistakes.

One reflection it offers us is that the transition to another form of production – another approach to the organization of the production of goods and services – is a long-term process. Capitalism has taken over four centuries to construct the material basis of its reproduction, in terms of creating a new way to organize labour, which goes hand in hand with technological development. Socialism had to walk with the legs of capitalism, without having its own material basis, and this had many consequences: the need for a surfeit of ideology and symbols; the establishment of an oppressive bureaucracy; and the failure to leave the capitalist mentality behind.

Another point to be made concerns democracy, and was well expressed by Lula, the head of the Brazilian Workers' Party, at a meeting of the Forum de São Paulo in San Salvador in 1996: any alternative to capitalism should not only be an *end* but must also be the *means*. A party, which is ahead of its time and espouses the truth, including philosophical truths, in what Marx would have called 'theological language', can only end up by suffocating democracy. Lula is clearly not talking about a form of democracy reserved for those who can pay for it but about one which allows people and social groups to express their needs and aspirations at various levels of real life.

Finally, we should be aware that the need to establish a power relationship to construct alternatives is also a lesson in contemporary history. We should not forget that it is the very existence of the Eastern bloc, with all its ambiguities, which incited Western societies, at least indirectly, to establish the post-war social welfare systems. The welfare state was a defence strategy against the danger posed by the threat of a more aggressive socialism created by the working classes. And the defence strategy had positive results. Social welfare was also the fruit of internal social struggles. Keynsianism was not born out of nothing. It came out of national liberation movements in the former colonial countries and revolutionary movements in countries like those of Central America, which forced the West to seek compromise solutions between a national bourgeoisie and the popular classes.

The fall of the Berlin wall shook this power relationship and the restructuring of the means of accumulating capital, which was at the root of financial crises and neoliberal solutions after the 1970s, only served to change the relationship yet further and more profoundly. A new power relationship must therefore be established, to allow for a response to the dismantling of the systems of social welfare and the weakening of social movements.

HOW TO APPROACH THE QUESTION OF ALTERNATIVES
When the word alternative is used in the plural it is not in an attempt to give an impression of a diluted mélange of small initiatives. There is one system which must be replaced, but there are also various different levels of change and varying times at which changes need to be implemented, not to mention the very many different places in which the changes will take place and the individuals in each of those places who will be working together to achieve that goal. This is why we must provide a detailed analysis of the subject.

Alternatives based on an analysis of social relations
What characterizes neoliberalism is the absence of consideration given to social relations. The market is presented as self-regulating for all social processes. The invisible hand produces a general balance on condition that the laws of the marketplace can continue to function freely (as a 'natural law' of the economy). The policies of structural adjustment are aimed at freeing the economy and cover privatization, the opening of the market, deregulation of labour, etcetera. All this is conceived in a social vacuum, with no consideration given to the relative weight of social groups. Under these circumstances we should not be surprised when the rich become richer and the poor become poorer; we should not regard this situation as if it happened by accident and can be rectified by taking various measures en route; we should see that in reality it is the very logic of the system which is causing the situation.

In any search for alternatives it is imperative to analyse existing social relations: the class structure, which is the direct result of the capitalist organization of the economy, but also the precapitalist: relationships between castes, different ethnic backgrounds, men and women. Without this analysis we cannot understand why, for example, in many countries in the South, neoliberal policies end up in caste conflicts (Africa, Chiapas) or in the feminization of poverty in the informal sector. This type of analysis is a vital precursor to any attempt to measure the social and cultural effects of the extension of the capitalist system, especially in its contemporary neoliberal phase. It also permits us to draw up strategies and alliances for resistance.

There is an important phase of delegitimization of the neoliberal system which coincides with the search for alternatives. This phase is based on the non-functioning of the human economy. In fact, in its current organization, the economy is not fulfilling its essential function of ensuring the availability of the goods and services necessary to all human beings for their existence. The human economy cannot be identified with either the theory or the practice of accumulation; or with competitivity; less still with the destruction of the environment and the exploitation of human beings. If, every five years, the United Nations announces that the number of poor in the world is rising, even in industrialized societies, this is not the result of bad luck but of the deficiencies of a system. Having noted this fact, which is essentially an economic one, one must move on to an analysis of the ethical aspect.

It is ethically unacceptable to allow the majority of human beings to continue living in materially, socially and culturally undignified conditions, at a time when humanity has never known so many possibilities for resolving its problems. A critique which is based only on ethical objections, however, can become an obstacle to true alternatives. First, it runs the risk of resulting in the criticism of individuals rather than of the system. A purely ethical critique can also be useful for the capitalist system, because it detects visible abuses but neglects the system's invisible logic, and thus contributes to the reproduction of the latter. And no system can resist its own corruption indefinitely, as was perfectly demonstrated in the case of real socialism. Every system needs transparency and control, including moral control, and ethical judgements thus need to be contextualized in a systemic critique to be effective.

So we need to integrate an analysis of social relations and a critique of the economic function, thus creating a different and visible logic. This was well expressed by Karl Polanyi, the American economist of Hungarian origin, who wrote about the need to re-embed the economy in society. Capitalism, displaying a genius indistinguishable from that of Walt Disney, has invented 'society' as a simulacrum in and of itself, and has ended up by imposing its norms and its objectives on all of society, where everything has a commercial value and we are heading for a total 'market state'. We have privatized everything right up to social security, not to mention development cooperation and public services.

WORLD CAPITALISM

What needs to be replaced by these alternatives is a massive construct, which is increasingly concentrated and interconnected, and increasingly beyond the control of the 'adjusted' states in its orbit. But the construct is vulnerable to its own contradictions: the disproportionate size of financial capital faced with the activities of production and services; pressure on labour income and the resultant crisis of under-consumption; the class divide, the bases of which cross borders. This is the context in which the alternatives must be conceived.

Different Levels of Alternative

There are many types of alternative. We have to try to clear the terrain and mark out the various different levels.

UTOPIA

We can dream of a perfectly balanced society, where the differences between individual initiative and solidarity are reduced to a simple state of tension, where human beings are judged because of what they are rather than the added value they produce, where cultures are considered to be equally valid expressions of being, and where scientific and technical progress is directed towards the well-being of all rather than the enrichment of a few.

We *must* dream of this type of society, whether we call it the Kingdom of God or a socialist society (why not even both at the same time?) because even if it is not attainable in our *topos* (place), it does have the force of attraction, mobilizing the spirit and the heart in this dream of the necessary utopia. But unless this utopia starts out from a firm conviction that it is *possible* to construct another social logic, and thus to approach the ideal, it remains a dream.

SOME BROAD OUTLINES

The search for alternatives passes through more general and realistic perspectives, while nevertheless being inspired by utopian ideals.

New initiatives in thought and action
After the demolition of socialism in Eastern Europe and the triumph of neoliberalism came profound disarray in alternative thinking. Some were seduced by the promise of liberalism: they hoped that economic gains might result, creating riches to be redistributed later; or they trusted in the idea of the indivisibility of freedoms, market freedom being the forerunner of other freedoms to come.

A further result of this demolition was the development of post-modernism in philosophy, the human sciences and, in particular, socio-logy. Starting out as a pertinent critique of modernism, scientism and totalitarianism in all forms, this movement reached the point of refusing to analyse situations in terms of globality or its systemic organization.

Instead it moved towards an overevaluation of the individual as the unique subject of current history at a time when capitalism had provided for itself the material and technical basis of a real world system. It should be added that there was a simultaneous weakening of the anti-systemic forces: unions, popular organizations, and revolutionary movements.

Little by little, new initiatives of thought and action saw the light. Across the five continents, many examples illuminated the new trend, particularly in the field of thought. There was resumption and growth in the critical analysis of Marxist thought and practices, and rethinking on the political left. The São Paulo Forum in Latin America is one example: it moved from a critique of neoliberalism and self-criticism by the Latin American left to a progressive formulation of alternatives. This was the central theme of the meeting in Porto Alegre in 1997. In Asia, People's Power for the Twenty-first Century (PP XXI) brought together social action groups and popular movements from all over the continent and went through a similar evolution.

All over the world social pressure is being brought to bear to demand democracy, which is increasingly seen as a methodological requirement that goes far beyond the simple electoral process. This is one of the main thrusts of the teachings of the Zapatistas in Mexico. We are also witnessing attempts to globalize resistance at the level of political thought. One example of this is the launch of the World Forum for Alternatives, with its headquarters in Dakar. But there have also been new initiatives in action, such as the Europe-wide strikes at Renault, in solidarity with the closure of one of the company's headquarters in Vilvorde, Belgium.

Redefinition of globalization

Rather than seeking globalization directed by the needs of capitalist accumulation, we should be aiming for a synthesis of regional groups: the European Union, Mercosur (the Latin American common market oganization) and the Association of South-east Asian Nations (ASEAN), all of which primarily represent an extension of the regional dimension of the market, but nevertheless also give real, even shared power to states to govern their own economies. This would provide states with increased protection against transnational businesses and would place them in an improved negotiating position *vis-à-vis* other groups. It would also allow the poorer states, in particular, to develop negotiating power on an international scale. Finally, groups of this kind would form the basis of the organization of collective security.

Regulatory mechanisms and institutions would accompany this type of reorganization on a world level, so as to ensure a balance in economic transactions, political cooperation and international security. The Bretton Woods organizations would exercise new functions whereby they would cease to be instruments of neoliberalism. This new regime would bring about a polycentric world, with a philosophy opposed to the current form of globalization under the domination of transnational businesses and capitalism. This is in no way to choose autocracy or isolationism, but to elect instead for disconnection from globalization in its current form so as to allow for the construction of a new form of globalization on a different basis.

Regional response to the real needs of the people
On the basis of the regional groups referred to above, the next step would be to work on the basis of auto-centred development – that is, development centred around the satisfaction of interdependent local needs rather than based on the current philosophy of everything for export. So these regional groups would not just be stops on the path to capitalist globalization – as in the case of ALENA, the free exchange zone between the United States, Canada and Mexico – but would act as poles of development responding to the real needs of local populations. In Africa, for example, this would allow for the promotion of sustainable agriculture supported by industrialization.

All this presupposes, of course, the development of regional policies inside each of the groups, capable of taking the necessary economic and social measures to ensure stabilization. In particular, mechanisms would need to be set up to strengthen the position of the weakest countries or social groups.

Alternative eco-development
The word 'sustainable' does the rounds today as a quasi-magic term, but in official literature it is used outside the context of social relations. This was the price paid to ensure the continued existence of the concept in a neoliberal world. This is why we prefer to use the term alternative eco-development. This term implies the creation of new relationships of social production, responding simultaneously to the impasse created by the destruction of non-renewable natural resources, pollution and ecological deregulation.

New social, popular and democratic alliances
In order to create the power relationships capable of achieving these political goals, we need to establish new, alternative social alliances. In industrialized countries, the time has come to work towards common strategies between the working class, the declining middle class, the intellectuals, the migrants and the movements representing specific

social interests: environmentalism, empowerment of women, children's rights, etcetera. In the countries of the South, faced with the alliance between international capital, the comprador bourgeoisie and part of the middle class, the alternative consists of joint programmes and actions to bring together the different grassroots groups – workers, peasants, the informal sector, movements of the urban poor, cooperatives, minority ethnic groups – and also the vulnerable middle classes, including students. Recent experiences prove that these broad social alliances are possible, even if nothing is ever permanent in this area.

Reorientation of international political powers
The creation of regional entities clearly requires political redefinition. European experience shows that the lack of political definition within the regional powers is one of the major obstacles to their efficiency. There is no doubt that this will require a redefinition of the sovereignty of existing states. But at the same time it will give back to these states more real power *vis-à-vis* the transnational economic powers, which are destroying their sovereignty even more effectively than any regional grouping ever could.

In addition, the political reorganization of the United Nations and its specialized organizations is essential. Some of these organizations have already been the object of retaliation by the leading neoliberal states. Take, for example, the case of UNESCO, from which the United States, the UK and Singapore have withdrawn with accusations of undue favouritism towards the less-developed countries of the South. Similarly, the role of the ILO has been questioned by the Unites States senate on the pretext that the fall of the socialist bloc renders it obsolete. It is true that the neoliberal dogma of total deregulation of labour is hardly compatible with an organization which supports secure employment and other welfare arrangements. The real goal we should be aiming for is the progressive creation of a world state, with a world confederation of states as an intermediate objective.

This is why the demand for a democratization of the international organizations is an integral part of the alternative. In particular, this applies to the Security Council, which is so dominated by Western interests. As far as the World Bank, the IMF and the WTO are concerned, they require total transformation to accord with a philosophy that meets the integral goals of the economy: the satisfaction of human needs rather than the promotion of capital accumulation.

Forms of democratic organization at all levels
The very concept of democracy is being rethought and extended today. Democracy is all too often limited to the concepts of multi-party political

leadership and the electoral process and is understood in these terms within the neoliberal discourse (but not necessarily in its practices). It takes on another meaning, however, in the context of new social movements and the building of a new contemporary politics. The central political issue is deepening and widening the way in which public powers function democratically. This is particularly true at a global or inter-state level. Furthermore, state decentralization – as in the importance given to municipal authorities and linked organizations such as the *panchayat* in India or CACES in Haiti – is a step forward, provided it is not conceived simply as a form of dismantling the state.

At an economic level, the various formulae for self-managing democracy are all valuable, particularly at the level of local initiatives or small and medium businesses. When it concerns large-scale production we need to seek other formulae, new forms of social links between workers that go beyond the joint management approach aimed above all at integrating them into the logic of capitalist accumulation.

On the question of democracy, it is worth adding two thoughts on the subject of terms often used these days whose meaning or interpretation has been altered profoundly by neoliberal discourse and practices. First there is the notion of civil society. This term is used by democratic institutions as well, but often in the sense given to it by the dominant discourse. In reality, civil society is the place of social struggle and the notion does not apply solely to democratic organizations and social movements. Transnational business lobbies that seek to influence national or regional parliaments are also a part of civil society.

So terms must always be used judiciously. From a neoliberal perspective, strengthening civil society can also mean destroying the state on the pretext of privatizing its services. If it is true that the concept is distinct from everything which relates to the public sector, it cannot be distinct from the reality of concrete social relations existing in a society and, thus, from social struggle. So the promotion of civil society is not a panacea to avoid conflict. On the contrary, it highlights the efforts of the weakest to organize a more just society and to overturn the existing power relations.

The second concept is that of NGOs (one issue of *Alternatives Sud* was dedicated to this topic in 1997). Within the framework of neoliberalism, NGOs are considered to be organizations capable of finding solutions to social problems. But this positive definition is situated within the context of aid to support the struggle against poverty, or as a response to needs not covered by society. As soon as NGOs move out of this perspective and support social or economic movements they are regarded with mistrust and the political and economic powers try to control them or to use them for their own ends.

There are two dangers for NGOs in this context. The first is that they may become, or be made into, palliatives to structural outcomes of the economic system, rather like the delegates at St Vincent de Paul conferences in the eighteenth and nineteenth centuries: fine people, but ineffective in the struggle to change social relations. The second danger is that, under the influence of established powers, they may become weighed down in bureaucracy and end up as centres of power themselves, forced little by little to subscribe to the dominant logic in order to reproduce socially.

The role of culture in social emancipation

All large-scale social movements have produced their own cultural expressions, diffusing their movement and their values and thus becoming imbedded in local culture. Then these expressions, in turn, are fertilized by social interaction. Social movements are expressed through poetry, music, painting, songs, theology and liturgy. A striking example of this can be seen in the Sandinista revolution in Nicaragua. But expressions of culture are only real if they grow in a democratic context. They cannot be imposed. They are a sign of popular authenticity.

HOW TO ACHIEVE THE GOAL

Talking of utopia is necessary and even good. But it is even better to draw up the broad outlines of an alternative project, even if this always remains provisional. The big question remains the method of achieving the project, and how to define the means.

The start of new perspectives

We should recognize that the debate in this area has only just begun and is still distinctly secondary to the institutionalized practices of the past: the logic of reproduction of the institutions (political parties, unions, state forms); the cooption of individuals or organizations from the popular sector into the dominant system (some unions, NGOs, agricultural cooperatives); the corporatism of social groups that lead individual struggles without placing them in the context of overall social objectives; the pragmatism of the left when it has achieved positions of power, losing sight of utopia and becoming too engrossed in conflicts of interest within existing society. In short, history weighs down with considerable force, but the importance of what is at stake forces us to take a different approach. And all over the world we can see the emergence of new reflections, proposals and experiences.

Today, proposals are emerging for a series of concrete regulatory measures and we will look at these later. None of these could succeed, however, without a social movement propelled by democratic and popular forces. Some see this as the only way of saving a regime rendered fragile by its destructive practices (notably financial speculation), discredited by its own mistakes, and endangered by social divides (internal and North–South). Others, on the other hand, find in it the means of moving forward towards a fundamental transformation of the economic system and its political expressions. In other words, for some, it is a question of neo-Keynesianism and for others it is the point of departure for a non-capitalist alternative to neoliberalism.

The areas in which regulations are proposed are varied. We will specify them without going into any detail, since each has been the object of detailed analysis and debate. Not only can they be interpreted from totally different perspectives, as we have said, but experts disagree on the concrete mechanisms of their implementation. In this document we will simply list the various regulations.

Economic regulations
Obviously, most of the major proposals fall into this category.

- Regulation and taxation of international financial operations.

- Regional and international fiscal regimes.

- Elimination of tax havens.

- Reduction of external debt for economically disadvantaged countries.

- Setting up of regions as sites of economic resistance.

- Transformation of the IMF and World Bank into regulatory bodies.

- World sharing of technology.

- Creation of new paradigms of political economy and socialization of the market.

Ecological regulations

- Efficient protection of non-renewable resources.

- Protective regulation of biological resources.

- Strengthening of the programme of the UN's Agenda 21.

Social regulations

- Labour legislation on regional and international levels.

- Participatory power for social and popular organizations in economic, political and cultural, regional and international institutions.

Political regulations

- Reconstruction of the power of the state as a regulatory instrument.

- Constitution of regional regimes with regulatory powers.

- Reorganization of international organizations: democratization of the UN and the creation of regulatory organs at this level.

- Global management of natural resources.

- Institution of a world parliament.

Cultural regulations

- Creation of new cultural consumer models, respectful of the environment and of the equal sharing of world resources.

- Creation of new models of agricultural production, which are non-destructive to the earth and groundwater layers.

- Conception of new models of industrial production, placing technology at the service of labour rather than accumulation.

- Establishment of a social code of ethics based on the analysis of local, regional and global social relations.

Social Alliances at the Global and Other Levels

Obviously such far-reaching objectives cannot be achieved, or even pursued, without a very demanding social struggle. While certain sectors of the dominant world economy realize that regulation is necessary to avoid the collapse of the system, most of them nevertheless try to support it and defend its integrity, identifying their interests with its reproduction. This is why the alliances that must be created between social forces will have long- or short-term perspectives, depending on the concrete objectives in question. It comes down to creating power relations to obtain precise objectives. One current example is the Zapatista movement in Chiapas, which makes no claim to power but demands an alliance of all social forces to democratize society.

Such an alliance should never lose sight of its ultimate objective, its utopia; it has to avoid being shunted down a revolutionary branch line or being content with reformism. Yet we live in a world in which a great many forces and strategies are emerging, each with an urgent need to find solutions to a crisis involving hundreds of millions of people: failure to integrate these struggles risks collective suicide.

Conclusions

History is a dialectical rather than a linear process. On an economic and social level it is the working out of two contradictions that affect modes of production. The first contradiction is that of the physical limits set by the natural environment; the second is that of the limits of any given system of human exploitation. Out of the synergy of these two tensions social struggles emerge to construct another system of production, another collective organization of humanity. The current transition can already be seen in the questioning of the social forms of an economy which every day has to struggle harder to reproduce itself; and in the emergence of social struggles with repercussions that go beyond their place of origin and also create new forms of organization. It is going to be a long transition period, but it has begun.

The inheritance left by the past in the area of social analysis, in the definition of collective objectives and the momentum of struggle, should definitely not be abandoned. A critical study of this inheritance provides a constant source of new lessons. Today, these lessons place the emphasis on long-term transition, on a multiplicity of strategies and on democracy as a means and not only as an end. It may be time for a renewed vision of socialism.

9

THE GLOBALIZATION OF SOCIAL STRUGGLES

SAMIR AMIN

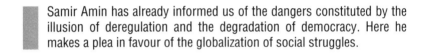

Samir Amin has already informed us of the dangers constituted by the illusion of deregulation and the degradation of democracy. Here he makes a plea in favour of the globalization of social struggles.

Increasing conflicts and social struggles

We have entered a new phase in this history which turns out not to have an end; it is a phase in which conflicts are exacerbated and social and political struggles are on the rise. The climate of uncertainty has already worsened contradictions within the dominant classes in the European Union, in Russia and in the countries affected by the developing crisis (Korea and South-east Asia, but tomorrow it will be Latin America, Africa, the Arab world and India). There are no guarantees that these contradictions will be resolved through democratic means. In a general fashion, the dominant classes are trying to avoid a situation where people take part in debates so that they can manipulate opinion (thus maintaining the appearance of democracy), or by planning outright violence.

These conflicts are beginning to take on international dimensions, becoming struggles between states and between groups of states. Already we can see a conflict brewing between the United States, Japan and their faithful Australian ally, on one hand, and China and the other Asian countries on the other. The roof-raising anger that awaited Vice-President Al Gore at the last summit of the Asia–Pacific Economic Cooperation Forum (APEC) in Kuala Lumpur is sufficient witness of this. It is not difficult to imagine the rebirth of a conflict between the United States and Russia if the latter manages to emerge from the tailspin into which it plunged under Boris Yeltsin. The conflicts between the European Union (or certain of its members), Japan and the

United States, which until now have been diplomatically managed, will also take on greater importance and the resulting tension will be vented on those who oppose the Triad, namely Russia, China, India and the Third World in general. Far from having contributed to reducing chauvinistic nationalism, neoliberal globalization has actually contributed to its increase.

At the same time the new phase is already characterized by the renewed and intensified struggles of working-class victims of the world system, whether these struggles are generalized or limited to particular class sectors, as in some countries. The list becomes longer every day: the landless farm labourers in Brazil, salaried workers and the unemployed in some European countries, trade unions uniting the vast majority of salaried workers (as in Korea or South Africa), the young and students encouraging the people of the towns (as in Indonesia), all are involved in the struggle.

The development of these social struggles seems certain. They will certainly be characterized by a wide-scale pluralism which is a definitive experience of our century (and a positive one for most of us). At the roots of this pluralism we should recognize the combined impact of what are sometimes called 'the new social movements': women, environmentalists, democrats on various fronts. The challenges confronting this development are of various kinds, depending on the time and the place, but we can try to outline the main opportunities for political action.

We need to define the elements of an alternative capable of uniting the various struggles at the national level, where the political choices are on the table. Linking aspirations to the democratization of society with those aiming to make the management of the economy accessible to the popular classes is probably the main strategy around which struggles can unite. This is such an important political pressure point that the defenders of neoliberalism will not hesitate to use their power to deflect popular anger into ethnic or fundamentalist cul-de-sacs.

But we also need to define the elements of a popular internationalism capable of giving a world scale to the struggle and thus contributing to the elaboration of a different globalization to that proposed by liberalism. The framework within which this has to be done is defined by the need to defend the sovereignty of nations while avoiding the one-way streets of nationalism. It is clearly on a regional level that this streategy can be built; whether these are pan-African, pan-Arab, Latin American or European constructions, they will share a socially progressive agenda and other cooperative regional projects.

However, we should not neglect action at the world level, which requires its own strategy. Politically, the aim is clearly to fight

American hegemony and its military arrogance. In this perspective reviving the role and the functions of the UN should be a common objective of democratic political forces. In addressing the reorganization of the economic system, we need to branch out from the well-trodden paths and the stifling confinement of the version of interdependence imposed by liberal globalization (the World Bank, the IMF, the WTO). The challenge consists in articulating the interdependence of trade in new ways (for example, by giving a major new role in international negotiation of these problems to UNCED), and in shaping monetary and financial interdependence so as to channel available capital in directions which allow the expansion of productive systems.

A framework of interdependence which emphasized the region (Europe, the Arab world, Africa) could also contribute to the construction of a pluricentral and non-imperialist world, opening up to the still-marginalized South and improving the chances of development, as long as this political evolution strengthens the potential for democratic and social affirmation of the people concerned.

The objective of our intervention at this other Davos (where we speak of the globalization of social struggle) is not to define action programmes to achieve human, democratic, social and equal development for the people of the world. Instead, the ambition of the World Forum for Alternatives, and all the organizations and individuals who wish to be associated with it, is to set up working groups on each of these themes, drawing together as great a diversity of analysts, and of social and political leaders, as possible.

10

A VERY DIFFERENT GLOBALIZATION

CHRISTOPHE AGUITON, RICCARDO PETRELLA AND
CHARLES-ANDRÉ UDRY

What are the main directions of the alternative programme proposed by Riccardo Petrella, Charles André Udry and Christophe Aguiton? This is their subject in the second part of their text.

Let us take control of our future. The world and all of life belong to all the inhabitants of the earth. Faced with the power of the social forces which dominate the global capitalist archipelago, appropriation of the future of the planet by its inhabitants will not be easy, nor will it happen overnight.

The expropriated people of the world have experienced this truth and are progressively becoming aware that they must focus their efforts, experience and innovation on another agenda of priorities to the one followed by the 'Men of Davos'. They are realizing that they need an autonomous method of thought and action to construct and promote their view of the world, of society, of ethical principles, of the economy, of social institutions. Finally, they are discovering that they have to prioritize their action, by identifying short-, medium-, and long-term working areas (and objectives to achieve). The authorities don't need to work like this. For them it is simpler: to ensure the longevity of their privileges, it is sufficient for them to be organized to exist.

The Priority:

A globalized welfare system, safeguarding a sustainable global ecosystem and the right to life for eight billion human beings who will inhabit the world twenty years from now.

The most significant and hardest social struggles taking place through-out the world are those concerned with *access to life*, to sources of life for the satisfaction of individual and collective needs for existence. This is borne out by the real conditions of the six billion people currently living on the earth and by the reports published in recent years by UNDP, the United Nations Environment Programme (UNEP), FAO, WHO, the World Bank, Amnesty International, Greenpeace, Oxfam and the ILO.

These struggles also engage with the occupation, use and distribution of the earth; with the right to eat, to have access to drinking water, and to be kept warm. They deal with housing, and with having a habitat fit for human beings. They cover the right to work, the conditions of work and the level of wages, and more generally the right to an income fit for a citizen. These are struggles for the rights of the child (International Convention of 1989) and in particular for the right to organize and educate the growing number of children in work; for the freedom of trade unions and the right to strike; and against company closures due to the search for greater profitability. They seek access to healthcare and to a basic education for all. They champion the basic right to exist, to enjoy a minimum of security in the case of illness and accidents, and to live in an acceptable fashion in old age.

Other issues at stake are democracy, life within a community, and the respect and recognition of the basic human rights of immigrants and refugees. There is a fight for the emancipation and the rights of women; against the many forms of sexual discrimination linked, among other things, to the gender-based division of work and tasks; and for equal rights between male and female. Finally, people are struggling for the protection of the environment and for the right of future generations to inherit an inhabitable planet.

This cannot be an exhaustive list, but the priority agenda concerns living, the right to live and the right to life. And in twenty years there will be eight billion people inhabiting this earth, two billion more than there are today. But the population on the islands of the capitalist archipelago will not increase. The two billion extra people will swell the population of the zones and regions outside the archipelago: the marginalized, disinherited regions. Even today, the richest 20 per cent of the population of the world account for 86 per cent of global consumption compared to 72 per cent in 1970. What percentage will this be twenty years from now if the priorities of Davos prevail?

Through the struggles in which they are engaged, the expropriated people of the world are defining a new anthropology of global life in the twenty-first century. The recognition of water as being under common ownership by humanity is the most immediate and evident symbol of this new definition, the first landmark of a new human geography. The same logic spurs the struggle to return financial resources to the service of globalized social welfare and the creation of common wealth in terms of goods and services necessary and indispensable for the satisfaction of basic individual and collective needs.

In the framework of this alternative agenda we can see the strategic importance of intervening in the debate over intellectual property rights (biotechnology, seeds, informatics) – key instruments of the owners of capital (and particularly finance capital) who over the past thirty years have assumed ownership or control of almost all available material and immaterial resources. It is imperative that we define a new generation of public patrimonial rights covering goods and services considered indispensable for survival and for the fair and efficient functioning of society and the earth's ecosystem.

Clearly there is one priority, composed of three closely linked components: access to goods and services required for the satisfaction of basic vital needs (water, for example); finance at the service of globalized social welfare; and the revision of intellectual property rights together with the definition of public patrimonial rights.

The Method

Start by networking innovative experiences and political, social and economic struggles for a different globalization.

Experiences and actions of this kind include the successful action to reconquer the earth by the farmers in Brazil or Madagascar, the initiatives for education and rural training of women in Senegal, or the exemplary battles of the South Korean workers who demonstrated the possibility of constituting efficient intervocational trade union organizations in the so-called emerging countries. Other examples are the efficient use of the Internet by the Zapatista movement in Chiapas, by Amnesty International, or by the wives/mothers/daughters of the 'disappeared' of Pinochet's Chile and by the mothers of Argentina's 'May Square'. Yet others are the halting of a water privatization project in Montreal and the foundation in the surroundings of Lima (Villa San Salvador) of a city of 30,000 inhabitants inspired by the principles of full employment, housing for all and the prioritization of public transport.

Consider also the struggle against the MAI for the cancellation of Third World debt; or the struggle against embargoes imposed by an imperial power, the United States, on entire populations who must pay the price. There are also the campaigns for the elimination of tax havens and the new initiatives for real change in the role of banks (eco-banks, neo-mutual banks). These are just a few examples of the many initiatives that should be networked. For this to happen, it is essential that the story of this globalization should emerge as a narrative written in and by the lives of expropriated people and those who are in the process of constructing a future of solidarity and sustainability.

Networks already moving in this direction are many and diverse in nature, ranging from radical political militancy to forms of moderate, reformist or humanitarian voluntary civil associations. Each network plays an important role, but it is time to tighten the links, to converge on a common goal while reinforcing the community of objectives, priorities and modes of action. The development of an effective and democratic world trade union movement constitutes an essential element of the convergence process.

In terms of methodology we should give priority to the pooling of innovative experiences and struggles centred on overcoming the capitalist archipelago and implementing a system of world political regulation. This should be entirely new in comparison with the United Nations system of inter-state relations and the economic and technocratic logic of the Bretton Woods system (World Bank, IMF, GATT–WTO).

Starting from this pooling of synergy (in which The Other Davos is only a start), in a relatively short space of time we can achieve the objective of defining, implementing and narrating the other globalization. Within three or four years, it will be possible to give growing political effect to a first truly planetary vision.

Action

Short-, medium- and long-term action sectors

In line with the priorities of the alternative agenda, the principal *short-term action sectors* on which we should continue to work while strengthening our synergy are:

- *the finance action sector*, including mobilization around projects from the ATTAC network; continuation of the struggle against the return, in any other form, of the MAI; the strengthening of action for the cancellation of Third World debt; the battle against the political independence of the central banks and the sovereignty of monetary policy; action for the development of a 'new bank', for local exchange rate systems and against the defiscalization of enormous wealth concentrations;

- *the work and employment action sector* involves helping children and working women in Asia, Latin America and Africa as well as immigrants and the long-term unemployed in the islands of the capitalist archipelago. In this perspective, while the battle for a radical reduction in working hours continues, the major objective remains full employment across the world and on a world level;

- *the privatization action sector*: this is a relatively weak sector where campaigns remain limited and insufficient. Priority must be given to mobilization against the privatization of public transport, electricity, gas and above all water. Opposition must be urgently strengthened against the privatization of education and social security systems as well as health. Various experiences in many continents of the world show that mobilization in favour of the reaffirmation or recognition of water, gas and electricity, of education and health, of urban and rail transport as common public goods and services is a strategy that pays off over time.

The principal *medium- and long-term action sectors* are:

- *The political regulation action sector*, or the globalization of politics and the state, is the logical extension of action sectors on finance and privatization. Mobilization should focus on the reorganization of the United Nations; the role of continental, supranational political integration, taking full account of possible regional continental economic synergies; and a response to the priority needs of the world population. In this respect, the risk is that the only veritable supranational continental integration in twenty years time will be European integration, which may well never realize its democratic, supranational political nature. The problem of the sovereignty of the nation-state will be at the heart of this action sector, and closely linked to sovereignty are two other questions: that of citizenship (over and above nationality) and of property (struggle against the private appropriation of material and immaterial resources by 'intellectual property rights'; the redefinition of state property; the development on an international, supranational and world level of new forms of socialization, public ownership and mutualization of property).

- *The collective, global social welfare action sector* focuses on the dissociation between income and work, world taxation, minimum community income and universal allocation: a collection of concepts, choices and orientations which, though all dealing with the same problem, express different realities and solutions, even opposite ones. The variety of local historical situations require respect for diversity, but it demands great clarity on the part of the promoters of the other globalization. Lack of clarity has never been the basis of coherent and effective action.

- *The media and education action sector*. As far as the media are concerned, in this sector dominant forces continue to accumulate 'victory upon victory' (whether in television privatization and programming, the concentration of shares or the growing commercialization of the Internet). It is time to get organized. The success of action to guarantee the editorial independence of *Le Monde Diplomatique* and *Alternatives Economiques* in France through the creation of two associations shows that solutions exist. Similar associations need to be formed to protect a growing number of newspapers throughout the world. Concerning the link between media and education, it is necessary to prepare to anticipate and direct the metamorphosis which is likely in the coming five to ten years. We must not leave it to the logic of industry, trade or nation-states to define and govern this change; it is indispensable to create citizen-based alliances linking the worlds of education and media. The future of sustainable development largely depends on this.

- *The denuclearization, demilitarization and peace action sector.* The peace movements of the 1970s and 1980s have run out of steam. A new generation of pacifists is being born, at a time when the United States is relaunching plans for massive military investment.

    We need to promote and strengthen actions supporting denuclearization, demilitarization and peace. One of the most significant tasks is the implementation of rules and of peaceful economic behaviour that goes beyond competition, rivalry, warfare and struggle over markets and for survival. The demilitarization of the economy is a necessary basis for the demilitarization of states and of society.

11

SIMPLY A QUESTION OF TAKING BACK, TOGETHER, THE FUTURE OF THE WORLD

ATTAC

(ASSOCIATION FOR THE TAXATION OF FINANCIAL TRANSACTIONS IN THE INTERESTS OF THE CITIZEN)

Here two members of ATTAC's scientific committee discuss the global financial system and how to bring it under democratic control, an object ATTAC exists to address. There are pertinent and realistic remedies but the fundamental pressure must be exerted by the united will of social movements, networks, citizens and policy makers to force the financial system to respect the elementary rules of harmonious economic development.

Financial globalization increases economic insecurity and social inequality. It bypasses and undermines popular decision making, democratic institutions and sovereign states responsible for the general interest. In their place, it substitutes a purely speculative logic that expresses nothing more than the interests of transnational corporations and financial markets.

In the name of a transformation of the world depicted as a natural law, citizens and their representatives find their decision-making power contested. Such a humiliating proof of impotence encourages the growth of anti-democratic parties. It is urgent to block this process by creating new instruments of regulation and control at national, European and international levels. Experience clearly shows that governments will not do so without encouragement. Taking up the double challenge of social implosion and political surrender thus requires a dramatic increase in civic activism.

The total freedom of capital circulation, the existence of tax havens and the explosion of the volume of speculative transactions have forced governments into a frantic race to win the favour of big investors. Every day, one hundred billion dollars pass through the currency markets in search of instant profits, with no relation to the state of production or to trade in goods and services. The consequences of this state of affairs are the permanent increase of income on capital at the expense of labour, a pervasive economic insecurity, and the growth of poverty.

The social conseqences of these developments are even more severe for dependent countries that are affected directly by the financial crisis and are subject to the dictates of the IMF's adjustment plans. Debt service requires governments to lower social service budgets to a minimum and condemns societies to underdevelopment. Interest rates much higher than in the countries of the North contribute to the elimination of national producers; uncontrolled privatization and denationalization develop in the search for the resources demanded by investors.

Everywhere social rights are called into question. Where there are public retirement systems, workers are asked to replace them by a pension fund mechanism that subjects their own employers to the sole imperative of immediate profitability, extends the sphere of influence of finance, and persuades citizens of the obsolescence of institutions of solidarity between nations, peoples, and generations. Deregulation affects the labour market as a whole, and the results include degradation of working conditions, the growth of workplace insecurity and unemployment, and the dismantling of systems of social protection.

Using economic development and job creation as a pretext, the major powers have not given up plans for the MAI, which would give investors all the rights and leave national governments all the responsibilities. Under the pressure of public opinion and mobilization of activists, they had to abandon plans to negotiate this agreement under the OECD umbrella, but discussions will resume within the framework of the WTO. Meanwhile the US and the EU continue their free trade crusade, pushing for the creation of new zones of deregulation at the continental or intercontinental level (examples include the Transatlantic Economic Project between Europe and North America, or the extension of NAFTA into Latin America).

There is still time to put the brakes on most of these machines for creating inequalities between North and South as well as in the heart of the developed countries themselves. Too often, the argument of inevitability is reinforced by the censorship of information about alternatives. Thus international financial institutions and the major media (whose owners are often beneficiaries of globalization) have been silent about the proposal of the Canadian economist and Nobel laureate James Tobin to tax speculative transactions on currency markets. Even at the particularly low rate of 0.1 per cent, the Tobin Tax would bring in close to $100 billion every year. Collected for the most part by industrialized countries, where the principal financial markets are located, this money could be used to help struggle against inequalities, to promote education and public health in poor countries, and for food security and sustainable development. Such a measure expresses a clear anti-speculative perspective. It would sustain a logic of resistance and restore manoeuvring room to citizens and national governments; most of all, it would restore the proportional influence of political rather than financial considerations.

To this end, signatories propose to participate or to cooperate with the international movement ATTAC to debate, produce and disseminate information, and to act together, in their respective countries as well as on the continental and international levels. These joint actions have the following goals: to hamper international speculation, to tax income on capital, to penalize tax havens, to prevent the proliferation of pension funds, to promote transparency in investments in dependent countries, and to establish a legal framework for banking and financial operations in order to protect consumers and citizens. The employees of banking institutions can play an important role in overseeing these operations and in supporting the demand for the general annulment of the public debt of dependent countries, and the use of the resources thus freed on behalf of populations and sustainable development (thus paying off what many call the 'social and ecological debt'). More generally, the goals are: to reconquer ground lost by democracy to finance; to oppose further abandonment of national sovereignty citing as pretext the 'rights' of investors and merchants; and to create a democratic space at the global level.

It is simply a question of taking back, together, the future of our world.

12

CANCELLING THE DEBT

ERIC TOUSSAINT

> The burden of debt on fragile economies is a situation which calls for citizen solidarity movements across the world to say 'No! We will no longer allow our governments to legitimate and support a system and institutions that have lost all capacity for respecting social rights and recognizing collective suffering.' So argues Eric Toussaint in this, the second part of the discussion on debt he began in Chapter 6.

Radical progressive policies are once again necessary and possible. A major shift in world opinion began to surface during 1997–8 following setbacks to the policies imposed jointly by governments applying neoliberal dogmas, the owners of national and foreign capital, and multilateral financial institutions. As citizens of South-east Asia, Russia, Brazil, Mexico, Venezuela, Argentina, Central America and Africa, many people experienced a deterioration of their living conditions in the aftermath of the neoliberal hurricane. For the 400 million inhabitants of the former Asian tigers and dragons, the IMF came to stand for 'I'm fired'. A large percentage of the citizens of the world (including people within Europe) have begun to question neoliberal policies.

Amongst some of these groups the questioning takes contradictory and confused forms. The weakness of the radical left and the submission of the traditional left to the imperatives of the healthy market (and thus to the owners of capital) leaves room in most countries for parties and movements which divert action and the mood of the population towards the search for scapegoats from foreign countries or different religions.

Successfully resisting the continuing neoliberal offensive is certainly difficult but those who undertake this battle are not without support and have enjoyed partial successes. The fact that the French government under Lionel Jospin decided in October 1998 to withdraw from negotiations on the MAI was the result of an opposition campaign launched on all sides by social movements, trade unions and political parties not only in France but elsewhere in Europe, in the United States and in the Third World.

The transnationals and the US government will find another way to implement measures to secure the free movement of capital for those who own it, but they have suffered a significant setback: it has been demonstrated that by mobilizing forces it is possible to pressure those in power to change tactic.

Another indication of the groundswell of change which began in 1997–8 was that the United Nations Conference for Trade and Development and the G22 countries declared their support in September 1998 of the right of countries to declare a moratorium on the payment of their foreign debt. UNCTAD stated:

Countries under attack could decide on a moratorium of debt servicing so as to dissuade 'predators' and gain a 'breathing space' permitting them to arrange a debt rescheduling plan. Article VIII of the IMF Statutes could provide the legal basis necessary for the declaration of a moratorium on debt servicing. The decision to impose a moratorium could be taken unilaterally by countries whose currency is under attack. (UNCTAD press release, 28 August 1998)

These two institutions (UNCTAD and the G22) certainly do not carry much weight compared to the G7, the IMF, the World Bank and the WTO, but by turning their backs on the immutable rights of the creditors, they show that governments on the periphery are finding it increasingly difficult to justify their acceptance of the neoliberal globalization.

The 1998 UNDP report made the basic point that a tax of 4 per cent of the wealth of the 225 richest people on the planet would bring in $40 billion. This is the modest sum which needs to be invested each year in 'social support' to guarantee *universal access* to *drinking water* within ten years (1,300 million individuals did not enjoy this right in 1997); to *basic education* (1,000 million people are illiterate); to *basic healthcare* (17 million children die each year from easily cured illnesses); to *adequate nourishment* (2,000 million people suffer from anaemia); to *sanitary infrastructures*; and (for women) to *gynaecological and obstetric care*.

This vast programme would cost only the modest sum mentioned above: $40 billion per year over 10 years (UNDP 1998: 33). Compare this also with other 1997 figures such as $17 billion on food for domestic pets in Europe and the United States; $50 billion on cigarette consumption in Europe; $105 billion on alcohol consumption in Europe; $400 billion on drugs; $780 billion on military expenditure; and $1000 billion on advertising (UNDP 1998: 41, 70).

The years 1999 and 2000 are a jubilee in the Judaeo-Christian tradition (which dominates the small world of G7 leaders). The jubilee celebration has provided a suitable occasion for reflection on the need for debt cancellation. With a new debt crisis exploding, it is time to mobilize action to support the complete cancellation of the debt of the peripheral countries.

It is also imperative to impose the tax on international financial transactions called for by ATTAC. As urgently, we should instigate an inquiry into the resources held abroad by the rich citizens of peripheral countries: in certain cases, expropriation of these resources should follow since theft has been committed at the expense of entire populations. In another words, expropriated wealth should be returned to the people. Furthermore, a one-off 10 per cent tax should be levied on the wealth of the richest 10 per cent of households of each country. Strong measures should be taken to control the movement of capital. There should be a general reduction in working hours, with wage guarantees and compensatory employment. There should be a guarantee of access to the land for all farmers. And male/female equality should be ensured.

These are just some examples of measures, incomplete and insufficient but nevertheless necessary, that need to be taken if we wish to bring about a positive change in the satisfaction of basic human needs.

PART III

FOR A DIFFERENT KIND OF DAVOS

The two first parts of this book have introduced the project of going beyond a critique of the route taken by global capitalism towards framing solutions and valid alternatives to it and, above all, towards sharing these with others. In this way another vision of globalization may gain the public exposure it requires to compete with and subvert the dominant consensual discourse. Our message has no meaning unless it is transmitted by actors all over the world. It is through joint campaigns, meetings, marches and counter-summits that we can both forge the weapons of the people's globally coherent counter-offensive and broadcast an essential declaration: that the time has come for an alternative globalization to emerge from resistance and struggle.

It is in this spirit that The Other Davos was organized. The following texts may help us to understand the nature and the aims of this alternative summit.

13

THE GLOBALIZATION OF RESISTANCE AND STRUGGLES

FRANÇOIS HOUTART

We begin by going back to look at the way in which the alternative Davos was planned and presented before its realization. François Houtart was responsible for its coordination.

Faced with the globalization of the capitalist economy and the social and cultural consequences this brings with it, opposition and struggle is growing but remains fragmented. It is important to combine efforts both in thought and action, and this is why coordinating initiatives are sprouting in the most varied areas of the world, all pulling together the international strands already in existence to constitute an active and multi-centred network.

Even though resistance takes many different forms (against the MAI, for the jubilee year in 2000, towards a Tobin tax, seeking alternatives, etc.), and even if the struggles are specific in their aims (farmers, workers, indigenous or coloured people, citizens, ecologists, women, the urban poor, etc.) and though the various coordination groups are numerous (People's Power for the Twenty-first Century in Asia, São Paulo Forum in Latin America, etc.), all of these have a common thread: they all work to highlight the unacceptable nature of the current economic system.

Admittedly the heads of the world economy are also becoming worried as they take stock of the situation, noting particularly the presence of the Asian tigers, the irrational growth of the financial bubble and the extreme poverty in the world. Some of them are beginning to understand that action must be taken to control the crises, to regulate financial transfers and the casino economy, and to fight poverty. But the initiatives proposed by the international financial institutions or their powerful economic allies, far from being motivated by primarily humanitarian principles, are governed by the need to create new conditions under which to accumulate capital.

After twenty years of neoliberalism – with its constant emphasis on deregulation policies, excessive privatization, structural adjustment programmes, a weakening of the state, the struggle against socialist solutions, the marginalization or eradication of popular movements due to the need for readjustment of the accumulation process – the logic of the economic system is leading towards a neo-Keynesian stance. At the same time there are proposals to involve voluntary organizations of all sorts (NGOs, churches, etc.) in an effort to soften the blow in the most affected areas of social life.

But while all this is taking place, the logic of the system itself is not questioned. This logic aims to liberalize the market so as to encourage exchange and increase riches. This theoretical vision does not take account of the fact that the partners are not equal and that it is often the weakest who pay the cost of these operations, whether their vulnerability lies in their class, their ethnic background, their gender, their lack of political power or their cultural weakness. What is worse still is that this same 'may the best competitor win' logic really means 'may the strongest win'. And hence the emergence of resistance and struggles the world over.

The answer is certainly not to promote a new 'International', but rather to use the means developed by the economic system itself (and used by it to maintain its power base), including the knowledge and information to which one has access via modern technology. This is why networks should be built and maintained, and why concerted intervention on precise subjects – or during meetings and decision-making processes – is so important.

This is the background to the formation of a group of four relatively young organizations who have decided to create a public forum on the topic: 'The Globalization of Resistance and Struggles: Another Davos'. They will take the opportunity of the annual meeting of the World Economic Forum, which meets in Davos, Switzerland and at which, every year, the world powers and their economic institutions (transnational and international financial organizations) meet together. The aim is not to get involved in the agenda of this forum, but to take advantage of its presence and its repercussions in the media to sound another note, giving voice to the social resistance movements and to critical intellectuals, while seeking alternatives to neoliberalism and the new modalities of accumulation.

Five social movements from different parts of the world met in Davos on 30 January 1999. These organizations were: the Movement of Landless Farmworkers (MST) from Brazil, a trade union group (PICIS) from South Korea, the National Federation of Farmworkers' Organizations (FENOP) from Burkina Faso, the Womens' Movement from Quebec and the Movement of the Unemployed from France. There was no desire to represent all the movements in the world, but simply to express in the strongest terms, through the voices of those present, a point of view held by hundreds of millions of men and women across the world. The distribution of income is coming to resemble a glass of champagne where 20 per cent of the richest in the world control 82.7 per cent of its wealth and the poorest 60 per cent share 4.5 per cent of income (UNDP Report 1992). This situation must change and it is not the magic wand of the market that is going to do that.

At the meeting with the grassroots movements were intellectuals who hold their cause dear and analyse the world economy from their perspective, since in order to provide focused solutions and offer alternatives it is indispensable to arrive at a diagnostic which can globalize problems. Without minimizing the importance of the micro dimension which is the focus of the work of so many movements and NGOs, it is nevertheless important to place these in the macro structures, and to be capable of making proposals on various levels. Giving due weight to economic factors, we should not forget the ecological effects, which will help to determine our future behaviour, nor the vital importance of cultural phenomena which at once construct capitalist hegemony *and* lie at the base of resistance and the possibility of alternatives.

The Other Davos thus has several objectives. First, it aims to amplify the voice of those who are protesting against the structural injustices of the current economic system; second, it aims to raise awareness that we can plan the future differently and lay down some guidelines for the construction of networks to improve shared information and action in solidarity.

14

THE OTHER DAVOS IN ACTION

ZÜRICH, 28–29 JANUARY 1999

So as better to grasp the contents of this meeting, to know the participants and understand the significance of the occasion, we invite you to take a closer look at the exchange of ideas which took place over several days. The meeting was only made possible through the work of Charles André Udry and his team. It took place at the various levels presented below through discussions and debates, all of which shaped the content of this meeting of social, intellectual and citizen forces against the 'global leadership' of the World Economic Forum at Davos. The first four sections contain extracts from contributions and debates which were held in Zurich, 28–29 January 1999, while the last section summarizes the declarations and responses made to journalists during the press conference at Davos itself, 30 January. These are transcriptions of video recordings made by Frank Millo and Victor Cohen-Hadria during the meetings in the two Swiss cities.

The Individuals Present

François Houtart (*session chairman*): 'We have here the representatives of the four organizations which have created The Other Davos initiative: Susan George with other representatives of the Coalition against the MAI; Doug Hellinger of the Structural Adjustment Participatory Review International Network (SAPRIN), Samir Amin of the World Forum of Alternatives and Christophe Aguiton of ATTAC. They are here to respond to your questions. I think that we are all sufficiently relaxed to be able to work in a "serious" and organized yet friendly and very informal way. We can now present ourselves to you.'

Susan George: 'François, that was a nice introduction. I am Susan George, I am a writer and I am here as one of the people representing

THE OTHER DAVOS IN ACTION

the coalition against the MAI and its clones. The friends here, from the same collective, are Jean-Claude Amara, Julien Lusson, Agnès Bertrand and François Chesnais. We immediately felt the need to join this organization. I am president of the Observatoire de la mondialisation, which is one of the members of the coalition against the MAI which now has over 70 members in France; we were also very active in the international coalition against the MAI. We won an initial victory but we have to keep going because the MAI is now springing up again.'

Douglas Hellinger: 'I am Doug Hellinger, working with a group called the Development GAP in Washington. The Development GAP promotes collaboration with partners in the South.'

Christophe Aguiton: 'My name is Christophe Aguiton, I am French, a trade unionist, but I am currently particularly active in movements against unemployment in France, with Agir Contre le Chômage and, at the European level, with the network known as European Marches against Unemployment, Employment Insecurity and Exclusion. And it is with this hat on that I am a member of ATTAC, like a number of other participants who will introduce themselves shortly. It is a new association, originally French, which was launched by *Le Monde Diplomatique* and *Alternatives Economiques*, in collaboration with trade unions, social movements and NGOs, and with the support of militant activists. I would like to say that in France, as in numerous other countries, this association enjoys very close links with others present here, in particular with the coalition against the MAI. What has happened in France has also been experienced in other countries. That so much has been accomplished *together* is for us a sure sign of what is about to happen at the international level. We hope that this meeting will be a first step towards the global coordination of these networks.'

Ahmed Ben Bella: 'My name is Ahmed Ben Bella. I am here because I have been in contact with the organizers of this meeting for a long time. Among other things, I am president of the Arab Congress which brings together the Arab parties. I work a great deal on Arab problems but also in a more general way at the level of the world system and in North–South relations, and I think that my experience enables me to deal with these North–South problems much more effectively. The 'North–South dialogue' is dead and buried. It is at the level of NGOs located in the North and South that contact must be established and the problems of the world system examined. I am one of those who believed it was necessary to have an anti-Davos. I virtually live in Switzerland. Every year we take part in this great celebration of capitalism. Every year we have a visit from 2,500 bankers and other economic decision makers who come to serenade us on the virtues of capitalism. Now that we are on the point of beginning the anti-Davos, I am happy to be among you.'

Mario Luis Lill: 'My name is Mario Luis Lill and I represent Brazil's Movement for the Landless Peasants (MST). I am very happy to be here because this meeting takes place at a very opportune moment; and also because it is necessary to question the prevailing model of globalization, which is extremely destructive for the smallest and the weakest in our society and particularly for the small farmers. As a representative of MST, I hope that we will be able to develop some lines of action, to find the means to put an end to this process of destruction engendered by the globalization phenomenon.'

Vincent Espagne: 'I am from the French Droits Devant (Rights First) association, a member of the coalition against the clones of the MAI. I work with Observatoire de la mondialisation, and thus with Susan George and Agnès Bertrand, the secretariat of this coalition. We are also here to express the thoughts and the voices of those without rights – those without papers, without resources, without homes, whose numbers are increasing. We are delighted to meet today with women from the Maghreb, and with the landless from Brazil.'

Samir Amin: 'My name is Samir Amin. I represent a number of different organizations. On one hand I represent the World Forum for Alternatives, which since its inception has wanted to see the emergence of an anti-Davos. Behind the World Forum for Alternatives there is also the Forum of the Third World, a much older organization, which has never believed that globalization or imperialism was anything new and which has always been active in the battle against imperialism. This is the reason why we think that the debate on globalization should not only be a debate on economic neocolonialism but also on the different political aspects of globalization. And I am very happy that Sid Ahmed has raised some of the problems of hegemonism and of the military arrogance of the United States in particular, as one of the fundamental elements of the constellation which represents the current globalization'.

Ousséni Ouedraogo: 'My name is Ousséni Ouedraogo. It is a name which is not familiar to most of the people here. But I am perhaps the easiest to identify. I come from Burkina Faso, at the heart of West Africa, and I am here to represent a peasant-farmer organization created in 1996 to represent, negotiate and defend the interests of farmers faced with certain trends, certain programmes, certain policies over which they have no control. Our organization takes the view that a farmer is not a production machine. The farmer is a citizen, a development partner. And agriculture is not only an economic function; it also has an ecological and a social role to play. It is within this perspective that we analyse the conditions of production. We think about the legislative frameworks and about financial questions. We must inform the producers about the programmes and the policies decided upon high, up there in the administration, and help them to deal with this information. We are also called upon to carry their viewpoints on the environment to other partners and to defend their points of view. Thus, when this forum was mentioned, we said to ourselves that it has the same perspective, even if we are working at the micro level. We are delighted to be here to share our experience and to discover at the same time a rather different winter climate. Thank you.'

Riccardo Petrella: 'At this moment, I am still an adviser to the Commission of the European Union. I am a professor at the Catholic University of Louvain and I am also engaged in militant activities with groups that include the Friends of *Le Monde Diplomatique*, the Forum of the Small Villages of the World and the Groupe de Lisbonne.'

François Houtart: 'I am the Director of the Tricontinental Centre at Louvain-la-Neuve, a centre of documentation and study on Asia, Africa and Latin America, which publishes the journal *Alternatives Sud*. My discipline is the sociology of religion and in this capacity I taught at the Catholic University of Louvain, Belgium. My work and teaching have often taken me out of Europe, to the United States, to Latin America, to Asia and to Africa. I have been heavily involved in solidarity movements with the struggles of the South and in numerous social movements.

After all the other participants had introduced themselves the session chairman, drawing together these different strands in his conclusion, reflected on the diversity they represented.

François Houtart: 'I have counted 19 different nationalities here, from various continents. Oceania is unfortunately not present in body but is certainly here in spirit. Truly, we represent a very great diversity. This overview session has allowed us to summarize the different approaches and the different places of which we are speaking. And it is this which, for me, is the fundamental richness of this group. We are talking about different places, but these places are actually complementary. This diversity is also the guarantee of the success of the work we will accomplish over these three days and the mutual lessons which we will draw from all this. Clearly we are not aiming to all arrive at a unanimous agreement on a certain number of positions, but to establish the convergence which could result in the long term'.

The Dynamism of Diversity

Victor Cohen-Hadria: 'How do you explain this convergence today from all these very different people with their very varied experiences?'

Ahmed Ben Bella: 'All these people, despite their differences, are affected by the fact that the world system, as it currently operates, does not work. So we all find ourselves on the same wavelength. As a citizen of a Third World country, I think that the development of the Third World is like a shipwreck. We say this with recent developments in Asia in mind. People say to us: act like tigers, but we are aware that we cannot oblige. First, there are the physical limits of the planet. If we consumed a tigerish volume of energy, what would become of this planet? And then, these so-called tigers are already showing signs of premature senility. And these dilemmas affect 85 per cent of the population of the South, which will become 90 per cent within twenty years, according to United Nations figures.

Given this perspective, something must be done. We have to change the economic system. There are also the wars, the embargoes which continue and the United Nations which is falling apart. We see countries bombarding each other instead of creating common objectives. These are all problems of development, of the future, which concern us. Our planet is a little village and even now it is not in a very good state. Unemployment is increasing. The lot of the South today is poverty. There are also migratory flows. This is a matter of interconnecting vessels. The Third World is a vast shanty town and in front of it is a grassy plain. At any moment, we will see an invasion of the plain! Because these people have no hope, particularly young people, since the Third World is young. People realize that the problems are the same for the North and the South. People try to contain the invasion. But they won't succeed. The army has already been placed on the Swiss border. You cannot stop someone who is hungry and believes he can help himself.'

Victor Cohen-Hadria: 'Do you believe that it is possible for there to be common objectives between those who are in the very restricted zone of well-being and good health, and those who are in the shanty towns of the Third World?'

Ahmed Ben Bella: 'The proof is that we are here. I believe that we haven't yet found each other (and yet I have known certain of our friends here since 1983). Yes, I believe there is a conjunction, a common approach to try and move certain things. I do not think that we have found the definitive responses. It is by approaching the problem over the long term that we will succeed. But I have no hesitation in saying that we have reached the limits of the liberal system. It has had its moment. It cannot manage the world economy, and in the South things are going from bad to worse. UN figures show that hunger kills 35 million people each year. Debt is increasing. Countries can no longer pay even the interest on this debt. Tropical illnesses affect one and a half million people whilst scientific research does nothing since research is dependent on profit. The pharmaceutical company Roche does not do research on malaria: they are insolvent. And then there is the game on the stock exchanges and in the financial markets, the global speculation game in which more than $2,000 billion is exchanged every day, of which scarcely 5 per cent represents the real economy. In other words, it is a vast casino. The small casinos have rules and laws whilst for this one there are none, thanks to the Internet. We hear about Brazil falling, perhaps it will be China next.... Today there are alternatives and the hunger which kills 35 million people should not be fatal.

The UNDP report appears on 15 September each year. The last one revealed, among other figures, that 400 transnational billionaires possess half of the wealth of the world. The wealth of only 85 of these billionaires exceeds the output of China: one billion, two hundred million inhabitants. The report says that if these billionaires were taxed 4 per cent, it would eliminate all poverty and health problems in the entire world. It is not that the earth cannot feed all the world. It is the management of the available resources, which is catastrophic. Increasingly now it is money which creates the system. In addition, there are no more customs officials, no more policemen and the Internet is beyond all control. It is true, we have reached our limits. The Third World is in the process of growing according to the principle that misery creates more population. There is a French proverb which says that the bed of misery is prolific. I am a member of the Third World and I have participated for a long time in conferences on this topic.

The Third World has its flags, its anthems, but absolutely everything is controlled by the North, even down to the simple but essential things. For example, when the North sells to us, it is they who fix the price. When we are selling, it is they who fix the price. For corn, it's Chicago, for copper, it's London, for coffee.... And the price of raw materials has fallen dramatically recently. It is this chasm which is opening up in front of us. And so at Davos these people, these 2,000 bankers and leaders of the world economy, come each year to celebrate the 'Great Mass' of capitalism. As for us, we want to organize our own little mass. We have to change things, like the rules of the United Nations, for example. I am a man of the Third World and I see that the embargoes, such as those imposed on Libya and Iraq, are all decided in the North! Libya was attacked by bombers, and after that you dare talk of terrorism? Three countries (the United States, France and the UK) create a no-fly zone in Iraq, without the slightest consultation with the United Nations....'

Jean-Pierre Papart: 'I would like to add a few things to this as someone who lived in Nicaragua during the 1980s. The International Tribunal in The Hague condemned the guerrilla policy conducted by the United States through the trickery of the CIA. The guilty party was ordered to pay $11.2 billion in damages for the acts of terrorism committed, but the US refused to comply. Thus we see that the world's policeman makes use of the United Nations but it does not respect the verdict of the United Nations when it affects itself'.

Victor Cohen-Hadria: 'They don't even pay their subscription....'

Jean-Pierre Papart: 'That is a secondary point. It is not just them. But they were convicted, they did not respect the judgements of the International Tribunal in the Hague, particularly concerning the use of anti-personnel mines.... I would like to say one thing. One day, I was the first to be called to a school where a child had stepped on a mine (there are mines in Nicaragua in several regions; there are even anti-personnel mines carrying the picture of Mickey Mouse). That is the CIA's gift to the Nicaraguan people, under the pretext of fighting communism....'

Social Movements: Witnesses from Various Continents

Ousséni Ouedraogo of the National Federation of Farmers' Organizations (FENOP), Burkina Faso: 'Burkina Faso is known in West Africa as a country which has a long tradition of peasant-farmer organization. Effectively, there are 22,000 peasant-farmer organizations at the village level which, since 1967, have tried to direct economic development from within their culture, opposing the imported production models.

This dynamism has progressively resulted in associations at higher levels. This process continued and then, in 1990, there was a big political and economic change. There was the devaluation of the CFA franc, a structural adjustment programme with the disengagement of the state, the process of decentralization. All this threw up new challenges for the farmer organizations which exceeded their individual capacities.

There was a willingness and also a necessity to join forces, to strengthen collective and individual capabilities in order to face this new challenge effectively. At the same time, an international association launched a study on the peasant-farmer movement in Burkina Faso and three other West African countries. This study examined the strength of the social movement, its weaknesses, its challenges and its changes in the new context. To carry out this study, some peasant-farmer organizations participated in a consultative group. The result was very pertinent for these farmers. The consultative group thought it necessary to share it widely with other farmer organizations and so five organisations took the initiative to share the results of this study and managed to mobilize commitment and technical support.

During a meeting in 1994 on the results of the study, the people were informed about the structural adjustment programmes proposed by the IMF in the agricultural sector. At the end, they said: let us create a body which will keep us regularly informed on national policies which affect us. That is how the idea of creating a wider structure was born. There were those who disagreed with the decision, saying that we did not have a mandate from our base. They suggested that we organize a committee to study the question further. Did we know what the functions of this structure would be? Did we know what form the organization should take?

So we set up a committee which worked for two years in the various areas of production over a wide geographical region, and which visited other experiments in Africa so as to make more informed structural and organizational proposals. The results formed the basis of the founding assembly of the Federation which I represent here. That was in October 1996.

The Federation thus created has the role of representation, of defending farmer interests in negotiations. It tries to influence policies, legal conditions and the production environment. To this end we try to give as much information as we can. The power of information! The organizations at the base are regularly informed of policies and the Federation tries to translate their aspirations and visions at the national level, so as to influence certain policies and programmes. Currently there is also a programme funded by the European Union to support the professionalization of agriculture. Thanks to the interventions of our Federation, we have been able to influence the approach and the management structure of this programme. We also have a training role in the economic and technical areas.

Currently our Federation intervenes a great deal in economic matters. In all sectors we try to encourage the producers to calculate the cost of production. How much does it cost the farmers of Burkina to produce yams? How much does the production of such and such a cereal cost? That enables them to make strategic decisions, to have a choice. Either I work in this sector, or I change sector. I continue to market my product here, or I change my trading partner. In 1997 this work led rice producers to "block" their rice, to refuse to deliver it to the national collection company which was buying a kilo of rice at a price lower than the cost of production at 112 CFA francs. Thus they were selling at a loss. This also encouraged the producers of cotton to stop their delivery of cotton, to negotiate better conditions.

This campaign also led the producers of green beans to negotiate new prices and other working conditions with their partners. This did not succeed and there were some farmers who refused to produce green beans for export to France. Burkina will not produce many green beans this year. This is all because there are some farmers who refuse to work at a loss. They say that they would prefer to produce potatoes or tomatoes, etcetera…. These are the sorts of battle in which we engage. It is true that even this is not without its risks.

At the beginning when we started building the Federation, the state's hand was forced by its financial backers, who said: "There needs to be civilian representation and approval of the programmes if you want us to fund them." In this way they used the peasant-farmer organizations as alibis. "We invite you to join us, we will put you on the steering committee, we will present you to the newspapers, we will get you on television" – and you will have understood nothing. After a day of meetings, they give you a 120-page document which you have to read and upon which you are supposed to take a position. It is impossible.

We have tried to transform this political involvement by seriously preparing our meetings. We began to express alternative points of view. The state began to reject us, of course. And their backers (and critics) the development agencies followed suit: they wanted to validate their approaches, test them, and have them accepted without question, but they saw that, in fact, we were not willing to play that game. We didn't want to be used like opposition parties. We defend interests. If the state defends the interests of the farmers, we agree with the state. If the state works against our interests, we won't oppose the state, but we prepare to negotiate.

Here is an example. There was a meeting to discuss a programme.

Just before this, a development agency contacted us: "we are aware that you are the strongest peasant-farmer organization and we want to meet you." It was even a Sunday. We arranged for the board to meet them. We met. They opened their briefcases to say: "Look, the meeting tomorrow is about this, that and that. We discussed this with your Minister and this is his position, but we think it is not the right one. This is the direction that you should take." So we said: "No! That will not work. Tomorrow we will see. If the minister takes a position which does not meet the expectations of the farmers, we will oppose." But straight-away, they replied: "No? Ah! Gentlemen, we have come here to help you." We said, "No, but let us wait." They then closed their briefcases and said: "We thought you would be more open for discussions. It is a pity…." We cannot be used to persuade our states to accept decisions from outside. It is just this sort of practice that we see being used to weaken our states *vis-à-vis* these financial organizations.

I have said that the role we play is not without its risks, because there are measures from time to time against the movement: restricting its activities, that kind of thing. In my country there is a proverb which says that if the snake gets bigger and older, it is because it is hiding. We are aware of our current weaknesses. It is a new structure; we need to strengthen it. We are aware of our fragility and know what we can negotiate at the moment and what we cannot. We are now trying to make alliances at a sub-regional level in Africa and at the international level. It is as a result of this that we have become part of a peasant-farmer platform bringing together ten West African countries. We have also recently had contacts with the European peasant-farmer co-ordination programme, thanks to Entraide et Fraternité in Belgium.

And in coming here I also hope to make contacts. I hope that an information framework will emerge so that we can have information regularly on what is happening at the macro level and how it may be translated into operational programmes at our level; and, of course, so that we can inform other people, analysts and decision makers, on what is happening at a local level and which could feed their thinking.

That, within the limits of a short presentation, is what I wanted to say about our Federation. I thank you. '

Mario Luis Lill of Brazil's Movement of Landless Farmworkers: 'The MST is a movement for those without land, the small peasant- farmers of Brazil who are struggling principally for ownership of land. Brazil is still a country of *latifundia* or large properties. No government has really succeeded in bringing about real agrarian reform and, for the moment, during the ascendancy of neoliberalism, the situation of the landless peasant-farmers has become increasingly serious because the large properties are beginning to recover a certain legitimacy once more.

This year, the MST will be 15 years old. It was born out of concrete actions, struggles for occupation of the *latifundia* in the south of Brazil. Following its consolidation in the south, it spread to the rest of the country; today, it is active in 23 out of 25 states in Brazil. Our principal form of struggle is the occupation of the *latifundia* but we have developed other forms such as, notably, walks. In 1997, one of the largest walks brought 100,000 people, peasant-farmers without land, to the Brazilian capital.

The MST is both a trade union and a political and popular movement. It is a popular movement because it works without affiliation, which means that anyone at all can become a member of MST. It is a trade union movement because it tries to intervene in the making of government policies at the national level. The MST is not only a movement to procure land for peasant-farmers who don't have any, but also a family movement, arising out of the efforts of men, women and children who are seeking to promote the integrated development of the individual. From the moment land is occupied, we try to promote the movement through rural cooperatives and we also try to develop alternative technologies. Neither the forms of production we support nor the alternative technologies we use are large energy consumers. Through these alternatives, MST tries to promote a form of production which is ecologically sound.

This new form of alternative production is not fully established right across the movement. There is still a certain amount of internal dissent over its application and so it is really something which is just in its early stages. One of the other areas of MST activity is peasant-farmer education (literacy and schooling): I should point out that the level of illiteracy in the Brazilian countryside stands at 40–50 per cent. We have established schools in the different camps and we currently have some 1,500 schools and 70,000 pupils. MST also has agreements with the universities so that courses at university level can be given to peasants and to other members of MST. MST also tries to care for health. We have set up health units, and we have health workers, nurses and doctors; pharmacies have also been established, as well as an agreement with a Brazilian institution which produces medicines.'

Robert Crémieux of the Movement of the Unemployed in France: 'First, I would like to say that since the beginning of winter, numerous homeless people have died in the streets in France and that this is a situation we have known for several years. I say that because I don't feel myself to be here as a representative of a rich country – France is usually considered as one, of course – but on the contrary as a spokesperson for the misery which exists and which long remained absolutely hidden. I am also here to speak for a movement of the unemployed – not an NGO or a charity organization, but a movement which is fighting for rights.

Finally, I would like to state that I speak here as the representative of three unemployment associations (AC, APES, MNCP) which have developed a unified approach over a number of years – a factor which helps to explain, I believe, the relative success of our movement. In order to speak of the Movement of the Unemployed in France, we need to say something about our associations, born at the beginning of the 1980s when mass unemployment had become a continuous and inescapable feature of social life. It is a characteristic of these associations that they were created independently of the trade union movement – a circumstance perhaps unique to France. For some time now, however, the three associations have developed a strategy of unified action with the fourth unemployment organization in France, the Committee of the Unemployed–CGT, a subsidiary of the leading French trade union, the CGT.

This autonomy which is a characteristic of the movement does not mean that we are totally independent of other social movements. Our engagement in unified action ranges beyond the unemployment associations to the trade union movement and to other social movements. Indeed, our development in France would not have been possible if we had not been part of a group, and if we had not been supported by the trade unions in general and by particular allies such as the teachers' trade union, the FSU, the SUD trade union, or the Confédération Paysanne, which has been at our side since the beginning. This is also one of the idiosyncrasies of the French movement. In recent times, being able to count on the support of the CGT has been important.

Beyond the trade union movement, in France what we call the social movement is a growing movement that is often based on specific demands: fighting for the right to housing, for example, or supporting the demands of those without official papers. These struggles are sustained by movements such as DAL, Droits Devant or the Comité des Sans-Logis. Our movement is unitary and one of its other main characteristics is that very quickly it has become European or international.

Since the 1980s the MNCP has been a member of the Urban Network of the Unemployed. While by no means militant, this initiative has been very valuable in building a network at the European level. Since 1996, the associations of the unemployed have been seminally involved, in France and in Europe, in what are called the European Marches Against Unemployment, events which have brought to world attention the presence of a movement of the European unemployed. In 1997, the

European March Against Unemployment ended with a demonstration of 50,000 people in Amsterdam. This was the first pan-European social demonstration and sounded the rallying call for a movement that has since found resonances in several European countries. Organized in the winter of 1997–8, this wider Movement of the Unemployed started in France but later had links in Germany, Belgium and Italy. It has established itself as a legitimate organization, partly based on the network of European Marches Against Unemployment.

Just why are we here today? There is a logic: we have brought our action to the European level because we think that unemployment is not strictly a national question; it has its origins in European economic policy and this in turn operates at a global level. If the effects of unemployment, such as poverty, are experienced today as a global reality, this is not an inevitability. Political leaders are meeting, at this moment, at the World Economic Forum in Davos. I am sorry to note that this Forum also includes, if somewhat haphazardly, some leaders who oppose the policies of unemployment and misery that are currently developing in the world. Our unemployment associations and our movement are participants in the network of struggle against the MAI treaty. As the MNCP, we are founding members of the ATTAC network and we will also be present and participating in the World March of Women for the Year 2000, now in preparation. At the European level, this World March of Women will be in Cologne on 29 May, on the occasion of the European summit, when the network of European Marches will organize a demonstration on the lines of that held in Amsterdam.

Regarding the alternatives, I believe that we are here to discuss them. I think that this is a beginning, since we have not come here with a programme. On the contrary, I believe that in the same way that we have seen a delay in the social movement's challenge to the neoliberal construction of Europe, so we are way behind schedule on globalization. We have left the field open for too long. Today is the point of departure both for resistance and for building an alternative. But how? I think that we have to start with our experience at the European level. We certainly need to start by looking towards a convergence of goals. We also have to find common demands. This is all possible, despite our differences. We have found, at the European level, that we can quite easily find a common language. Here today, let us begin a dialogue to reveal the coordinates of an alternative.'

Sanggoo Kang from PICIS (Policy and Information Center for International Solidarity), Korea: 'We work to help KCTU and other trade union organizations to build international solidarity. Our problem just now is the liberal adjustment in Korea. KCTU itself was expected to be here, but an upcoming election in March is keeping them very busy and at present they have just one person in charge of international solidarity. But I know you are very interested in the upheaval experienced by Korean workers last year. As for this year, KCTU is planning a number of campaigns. Let's explain the situation. Since 1996 the Korean government (and three of its prominent members especially) has tried to institutionalize a radical neoliberal programme of privatization and deregulation of the financial market. They tried to effect their plan through legislation in the national assembly but as you know Korean workers struggled against the bill they introduced and finally it was posponed to the year 2000. Despite that decision in 1997, and the departure of one of the key pro-liberalization members, other government members continued to promote the policy, insisting that foreign direct investment in Korea was the only viable road to economic survival. Eventually they came up with a reform proposal of liberal laws based on a lay-off and dismissal system that was agreed in a committee session of the assembly, with support from the Federation of Korean Trade Unions (FKTU), which backs the government.

Following the agreement there was massive retrenchment in Korean industry. Unions fought fiercely against the lay-offs last year. The strike went on for three months, during which time workers were subjected to violent repression by the police. At Mando Machinery factories a force of 17,000 police invaded the area and arrested many of the workers. The main issues last year were the lay-offs and social security. Korean workers depend on a single wage and there is no social safety net. They therefore have an urgent case for human rights at a basic workplace level.

In the view of many workers and other Koreans the struggle between the union organization and the companies was not successful. We think it was at least effective in restraining the scale of retrenchment and redundancy. Now there is at least a foundation for continuing protest against high unemployment and the pressing need for social security.

In the second part of its legislative programme, the government announced a two-stage plan (July and October) of public enterprise privatizations and management renovation. The first stage included 11 enterprises and 21 affiliated companies, representing 30 per cent of all public enterprises – but 70 per cent in terms of employees and total sales. Key national industries such as Poahan, the Iron and Steel Corporation, the Korean gas corporation, construction companies and telecommunications operators are all included in the plan. Workers have found it difficult to resist because of a history of corruption involving collusion between the government and capital under the military dictatorship. Most people believe that public enterprises were rotten and that the only way to stop the rot was to privatize them. This is now government ideology and many people support it – making it difficult for the workers to oppose the sell-off.

The third government legislative initiative was the deregulation of financial market such as stocks and bonds. Foreign investors were quick to respond, seeing a profitable opportunity. Because it pleased the IMF, many people thought that opening the market was very important for Korea's future. Although Korean workers and their unions have fought this neoliberal structural adjustment, it has been an uphill struggle.

The decision to embark on a general strike was postponed and then approved again during the last year, with parliament proving very persuasive. KCTU has insisted on dialogue to solve the problem, believing it can repeat its victory against the government. This year parliament decided to complete the structural adjustment process in Korea, announcing the Big Deal as part of its plan. Big Deal involves Sanson Waters giving its motors department to Deo, and Deo handing its electronics department to Sanson: in this process, however, workers are completely excluded and they have struggled fiercely against Big Deal with the help of KCTU. Their first objective is security and stability; their second is to organize and unify workers to battle against the threat of unemployment. The strategy is to politicize and strengthen solidarity with social movements and activists abroad. Solidarity meetings are planned, and certain groups are preparing to protest against deregulated investment agreements and capital flows.'

François Houtart: 'After having listened to these statements, I am struck by two things. The first is that the North–South divide is real in its forms but artificial in its logic. We are indeed dealing with a world system. The second point is that right now there is a convergence of objectives among very diverse movements, and that some impressive interactions are taking place.'

Convergent Struggles and the Evolution of Capitalism

Christophe Aguiton: 'I would like to make some proposals in the name of ATTAC, and in the knowledge that they are already being discussed in other collectives. We can make a double observation. First, we can observe the embryonic but real beginnings of a coordination of struggles and movements on the continental and international levels. We have seen the European level in play with the European Marches, but also in worker struggles such as those at Renault Vilvorde and in trade union demonstrations like those organized by the European Trade Union Confederation.

On the American continent, regular conferences take place every time the heads of state sit down to liberalize the market, from Alaska to Tierra del Fuego. Similar meetings are taking place in Asia, and we should also note that international coordination is being established and is beginning to gain ground. The collective action against the MAI is the latest illustration of this and has gained a first, symbolically important victory, even if it may prove to be short-lived.

The second aspect of the observation is that there is evidence of a link, even if it is not direct, between this upsurge of coordinated struggles and movements, on one hand, and the economic and political evolution of the world in recent years on the other. Medium-term changes like the general opening of the market – in goods or services, in financial services especially, but even in labour – are accelerating the transformation of the capitalist system, with significant social consequences for all regions of the world.

In the South, of course, among the peasant-farmers, the battle against the patent on life forms, and against profit-driven genetic engineering such as the infamous "terminator" seeds, is one of the most advanced signs. Change in Eastern Europe has seen the collapse of whole countries, Russia included. But there is also a negative evolution in the developed countries themselves. This can be seen in the demise of labour contracts or, at the very least, a general weakening of the once stable and fixed labour contract – once the norm in the richest countries – and the general rise in uncertainty and unemployment; for those still working, this has brought a deterioration in working conditions in the guise of what is called "flexibility".

These are the social roots from which stems the willingness of different social movements to take their own affairs in hand at the local, but also at the continental and international levels. These are all medium-term evolutions, to which can be added – as reflected in the concerns of this meeting today – short-term evolutions. For the crisis which started a year ago has had direct effects. ATTAC, for example, only exists because a certain number of people and *Le Monde Diplomatique* declared that, in the face of the economic, political and financial crisis, it was essential to take things in hand.

A major financial and economic crisis is beginning, with deflation in countries such as Japan having major effects on countries such as South Korea and Brazil but also on developed countries which are starting to move into recession. In the light of our double observation, we would like to float an idea and make a proposal. Is it not time to start co-ordinating our resistance and struggles on an international level? Isn't it time to unite in the face of the social effects we have been witnessing, especially those resulting from the crisis? This is what we want to discuss today. We think that this Other Davos is the first sign. But we would like to render this first stage of coordination more concrete and more stable. For us, the *social* aspect is a determining element, more so than the *political* redefinition of the world. Of course, we are aware that without the American victory in the Gulf War in 1991, the world would not be what it is. The US used the prestige of its military victory to impose a redefinition of the world market, whether in agriculture or in the tradeable goods of the so-called information society.

Yes, we know that politics is 'behind' all this. But the movements that have emerged at an international level are looking at social questions, and we believe that it is important to use this as a starting point. Let us begin by saying straightaway what we think is impossible, and what we do *not* wish to do. We do not want to launch into an ideologically determined political International, which would turn us into a minority. This is not the proposal offered today, nor is it the objective of large associations which ATTAC represents, and which we are trying to build at all levels. But we do believe that it is useless and a mistake to try to compete with or replace that which already exists.

There are NGOs that do useful work and there are international structures that are effective, even if we may debate their direction and their actions. This is the case, for example, in the agricultural sphere where Via Campesina is active, or in international trade unionism, whatever the various criticisms that can be made about this or that structure. There *are* structures which would benefit from change, improvement or revitalization, but we are not about to compete with them or replace them. What we are proposing is *coordination*, which would permit two things. First, it would help us to understand what has happened in each of our countries – why particular struggles have developed, what the factors are behind their success or setbacks – and to learn from each experience. Second, we want to try to act together and we think that it is through joint action that we can stabilize the long-term network coordination that we are looking for. And we would like to propose action in four areas which appear to us to be key and in which it seems possible to act.

The first area is international treaties. Clearly this includes the MAI as far as its foreseeable future is concerned, but also the Transatlantic Economic Partnership, WTO and all the initiatives that will be tomorrow's regional or international treaties, with potentially harmful consequences for the living and working conditions of people everywhere.

The second area is Third World debt, the theme of activists for decades now but also very topical today, with campaigns being launched by others apart from us. I am thinking here of Jubilee 2000, which was launched by the Christian Churches. Even if many of us would find their demands a little too limited, since they propose debt cancellation only for the poorest countries and not for economically important countries such as Brazil, action in this area appears essential.

The third area is the agenda of the international institutions and, top of the list, the plans of the IMF – the consequences of which we have seen in South Korea, Brazil and in numerous other countries where international solidarity could be vital.

The fourth area is one on which ATTAC has concentrated: financial deregulation. Here the aim is to tax free-flowing capital, but also to attack the proliferation of pension funds and to expose and combat the important role tax havens play in the world economy. The general aim of all these measures is to recuperate funds which could go instead to the victims of the system, to the poverty-hit countries of the South and to the unemployed in the rich countries.

Perhaps we might add *a fifth area*, very broadly defined at this stage, but useful because it describes an aspect not only of the desired future but also of our means of getting there. This area is simply the defence of all social and democratic progress, in the recognition that only the broadest social support can ensure the success of our network co-ordination strategy.

Plainly the work of lobbying and convincing people is important. Of course many NGOs do very good work, and this work must be defended and extended. But our strength will come from the farmer associations, the trade unions of wage earners, the movements of the unemployed, the homeless, and those without official papers who are fighting on every continent. And that will be the key, in our view, to what we can implement together. There is a dilemma here and I highlight it as a first difficulty we have to overcome. We represent two realities, that of the NGOs, but also that of the social forces. We all know that in Northern Europe and in the United States the trade unions are rarely present in alliances such as ours, and that this is one of the things we aim to change, one of the challenges we face. We have to bring together *all* the social forces, including those in countries where associations and NGOs are more active than the trade unions, which tend to be professional or sectoral in their focus and to neglect issues of solidarity.

My conclusion: what practically should be done? We think that we must announce the launch of this coordination movement tomorrow at the press conference. We should use this public event as the day of the birth of this movement – and this should be the sense of the text that must be developed – since it is also the day for the public launch of this year's Davos vision.

And afterwards, we have to have more meetings. To start with, we could base this on what already exists. There are interventions already planned which, I think, would welcome a link with us. I have in mind the Permanent People's Tribunal which will hand down a judgement on the transnationals, starting with Elf, and undertake other initiatives. I am thinking of the Counter-G7 planned for Cologne in June. Thus we could plan our work around existing initiatives.'

Samir Amin: 'The wish expressed by Christophe, that our objective should be to help coordinate social struggles at the world level, is evidently an extremely ambitious and long-term objective. But it is never too late to start and it would not be a bad thing to start today. Only I do not expect that today or tomorrow we will make much progress in this direction. The problem is more complex than we think. Since the phase we have entered is not only a phase of growing social struggle, or even the struggle of classes in many countries of the world, but already a phase of increasing conflict between ruling classes – that is, between states. As a result, intervening in these conflicts and supporting social struggles, and possibly coordinating them, has a *political* dimension.

This is why I think that we should introduce this political dimension forcefully at Davos tomorrow. The people meeting in Davos and the journalists present represent the powers which are in conflict. And it is faced with these growing conflicts that there is a certain disarray in the opposing camp, with a certain number of concessions already planned. It is on this basis that I think it useful to bring to the attention of this discussion and of the editorial committee a document whose content I would like to see taken into consideration:

> The global system that we are fighting is not only a neoliberal economic system aiming at subordinating all social interests to the unilateral rule of capital. It has also a political dimension. The politics of the liberal economy aims at maintaining the maximal control of the triad over the rest of the world. To be efficient, this control must be based on reinforcing the political and military hegemony of the US. It must also contain the eventual conflicts of interest amongst countries of the triad within the frame of normal mercantile disputes, without bringing their fundamental agreement into question. That overall political strategy therefore aims at destroying any attempt by any society outside the triad to develop an oppositional potential – economically competitive, or politically, militarily or ideologically independent. It does not allow any development other than that which is fully or maximally controlled

by the triad. This focus on politics may throw a light on major recent events such as: (1) the attempt by the US and other triad powers to take advantage of the financial crisis of Korea, to dismantle its productive system and enforce its submission; (2) the strategy developed towards the ex-USSR and Russia, systematically and successfully aimed at destroying their industrial capacities; (3) the concessions which the G7 is now considering in order to maintain its overall control of the global financial system, threatened by the withdrawal of eastern, southern and south-east Asian countries from financial globalization and the possibility that Russia and some Latin American, African and western Asian countries may move in the same direction. The announcement of these concessions, such as the regulation of financial transfers, must be considered, meanwhile, as a defeat for global capitalism's project of total domination.'

Susan George: 'The coalition against the clones of the MAI has enjoyed undeniable initial success. The MAI, as presented at the OECD, is dead – and this is the fruit of coordinated work, not only in France but internationally. At our Vincennes meeting at the end of October 1998, 23 nationalities were represented. Ours is an example of a movement formed in an astonishingly short time, since our action only began in February 1998. And I believe that this success has brought two things: on one hand, it has opened a breach in the neoliberal consensus. This caused "a moment of panic" for those who discovered that they could no longer make treaties in secret and then have them approved by parliament. On the other hand, it has opened up a field of new possibilities for the social movements.

Our priority during this period of neoliberal reaction to our victory is to fight the clones of MAI which are already springing up. Immediately, we must counter the transfer of negotiations on investment to the WTO, in the Millennium Round, which currently has no legitimacy (it is the dream of Sir Leon Brittan), and their furtherance through the agreement known as the Transatlantic Economic Partnership. For us this is an urgent task, since if these two developments are to be implemented it will be before the end of the year. Everything is already planned by the opposition and we think that implementation will be a setback for all types of struggle. It will secure a package of framework laws which will make our struggles very difficult.

What we expect from this meeting is, first, work-sharing. It is increasingly difficult to be up to date on dossiers of extreme technical complexity. Yet the analyses need to be expressed in the language of the people. We must not be imprisoned by our ideology. We need to link research to social movements.

We emphasize this dimension – the sharing of work between researchers, analysts and social movements, with a constant dialectical movement between the two – and we need instruments for what we call the "pedagogy of the possible", since many things have become possible, but stand in need of instruments to enable them to be implemented. We have begun with a document, ASPIR, which combines analysis with a certain number of propositions. An Internet website has enabled us to monitor interest in this. On the other hand, we emphasize our relationship with the movement of those "without", "those without official papers", "the homeless", "those without rights". This movement provides the strength for what we have done,which is to show that an international treaty, while appearing abstract and difficult, is in reality a concrete fact for people who are really suffering. We have a long way to go in developing this relationship but we want to move ahead as fast as we can.

We have developed the habit of working together. The threat is world-wide and so the response must also be world-wide. We expect that this meeting will be able to build a consensus just as the men of Davos are doing on the other side, in the neoliberal domain. We hope to be able to sustain the struggles of the various groups by maintaining the emphasis on reciprocal support. When we introduce ourselves, for example, as the movement against the clones of the MAI, we want to be able to represent the Brazilians, the Koreans and so forth in the coalition. There is a division of work, too. We don't expect everyone to invest time in studying all the dossiers. We are supporting the June 1999 meeting in Paris as a French coalition. This meeting is an instrument of consensus and mutual support, and a meeting for future action, never forgetting that it is possible. We have already recorded a major victory and we can build upon this.'

Dario Lopreno from Asile, the organization of Swiss churches for the reception of migrants: 'One remark which may seem marginal, but which seems to me important, is that we should be *prudent*, even if I fully support what Christophe Aguiton just said. Personally and frankly, I doubt very much that the MAI agreement fell due to popular opposition. I think that popular opposition was a partial and marginal factor (even if it was a dramatic one, and important for that reason). A more significant factor was that the dominant classes and transnationals are not yet ready to move to such an advanced 'meta-national' level. That is the reason for the setback. We should not be contemplating our navels and patting ourselves on the back, exaggerating our strength....

The other problem, I think (and this is not the result of the manic depressive side of my profession, as someone who works in Asile –

"refuge" – an organization dealing with migrants) is that we must add to the central preoccupations of our thinking the question of refugees and asylum. This is becoming a crucial issue in Europe. When two thousand Kurds disembark in Italy we have the impression that there are millions of people landing everywhere at the same time, but this is nothing compared to the problem of asylum and refugees in the Third World. Europe receives only a tiny percentage of the refugees in the world. There is a very delicate irony which places us face to face with the ambiguity of the situation: the Iraqi refugee who arrives in Switzerland is loathed quite as much by the population, by the mass of Swiss people, as is the representative of the Iraqi government.

And a final thing, I think that it is important to reach agreement on the five points proposed by Christophe Aguiton. But I am not sure that on the fifth point, the defence of all social and democratic advances, we will all easily agree. I think that we could easily find divisions and disagreement. There are people who defend certain systems that are as ambiguous as those they attack and I think that this issue should also be at the centre of our debates. The question of the "synthesis" for me comes down to Riccardo Petrella's stress on the "common good" (see p. 102), which constitutes the encompassing principle of these five points. The presentation which I believe showed this most perfectly was that of the MST representative, who really showed to what extent the issue of the common good was behind all he presented. It was admirable and I propose that the text tomorrow reflects this aspect, which I think is a priority.'

Riccardo Petrella: 'I think that this meeting is important since little by little we are seeing, each in his own context and in his day-to-day experience, that we can create stories which are different from those of the dominant system. It seems to me that our strength can be further reinforced through other meetings of the same type which will follow. The dominant system has two extraordinary strengths. The first is the mastery of language: of analytical discourse, which tells us what is happening; and also of normative discourse, which tells us what to do. Let us take an example: the world is convinced that we are living in the knowledge society. We are told that we live in a knowledge economy, that we live in the information society. We are told that we are in the digital economy. And the majority of people, us included, have accepted that. And we use the same language. We are trapped and dominated by their mastery of the story.

The second force is the mastery of the ownership of means. Little by little, thanks to the system of intellectual property rights, they are in the process of taking everything. They have taken possession of the seed;

they have taken the land. Now Microsoft will take the inheritance of the photographs of the world. And little by little, they are taking our genes: human genetics, vegetal genetics, animal genetics. So intellectual property rights are the most extreme form of power over all the means and all the resources of the earth that global capitalism has acquired. We must fight against these things. And I hope to contribute over the coming months to the collective process of "consensus building" (Susan George) around an as yet untold story.

Of course, our story should be in the plural, not in the singular like that of the dominant power. And it should be built around three topics. The first is that of common goods and services. Have we, the opponents of capitalism, said anything about this? What do peasants in Brazil and bureaucrats like me from the European Community have in common? Can we provide common services to each other? Can we talk of common wealth? Can we justly claim that the historic function of the next twenty to thirty years, and of the global social struggle, is to create common wealth, and common basic goods and services, in terms of water and of food? This is the first topic. Do we have a different story from that of the dominant powers on this topic, concerning goods and services and wealth? In this framework we should be thinking seriously about the notion of property. What is property today in the contemporary world?

The second main topic is that of political representation. We, too, are in the process of simply accepting that parliaments are dying and losing their power. And yet, in our Western societies, if not perhaps in other societies, political representation goes through parliaments. Many of us – and many of our opponents – laugh when people talk of a world parliament. We do not believe in it. Is it good not to believe in it? Aren't we playing the game of the dominant powers if we accept that political, economic and social representation is difficult to implement at the world level? Are we not accomplices of the dominant system when we conclude that there is no way – such as democratic, direct representation, for example – to organize democracy with state systems?

The third topic concerns science and technology. All the forces of the Left have surrendered the discourse on science and technology to the dominant powers. There is no real autonomous conception by world opposition groups in the area of science and technology. All analysis dealing with politics, science and technology today is from the same mould, that of the dominant powers. We, the opposition, speak only of diversity in terms of using science and technology differently. But in terms of the economy and sociology of science and technology, or the anthropology of knowledge that applies in these spheres, we do not have a different discourse from the dominant powers.

So, we have three main areas on which can work with the diversity of approach which is our characteristic. And of course we must start with this fundamental approach of defending all social, democratic advances in the world. This is a fantastic resource. It is our common capital of the history of humanity, and we must support it.'

François Houtart: 'It is always a pleasure to listen to you, Riccardo, even if Italian notions of time are not the same as Swiss.'

Riccardo Petrella: 'There is a Rwandan proverb which says: "God gave the watch to the Swiss and the time to the Africans". Let us just say that I am a Swiss-African !'

François Chesnais: 'I believe that it is important to understand what is behind this process which leads us to the "common good" of the workers, the peasants, the unemployed and the intellectual workers. We have to take account of the fact that they are increasingly faced with the same problems, in the framework of the globalization movement which has links in every country. On top of global dualization one must add the internal dualization of each nation. And it is most prominent in the capitalist countries themselves. It is that which drives us to converge more and more.

On the topic of democracy and its current reconquest, I am on the side of those who are prepared to say that the start of democracy is the invasion of those places where decisions are made. I think that the rehabilitation of democracy will come through the most elementary expression of this desire by those at the bottom who invade such places; and all of this converges to find affirmation when faced with the places where decisions are taken. But next, it is not enough to say that we are facing a system of inequality. We are facing a system which, in the name of increasingly concentrated private property, is in the process of expropriating, not only the property of other people, but also those things which are so basic and vital that no one so far has had the effrontery to lay private claim to them.

We have arrived at a time in the social and political history of humanity when this private property which once served to fight the old regime has now transformed itself into something which we should challenge politically and conceptually. We can no longer be equivocal about questioning the private ownership of the means of production, ideas, seeds, water, etcetera, because this private ownership subjects us, in its name, to aggression every day of our lives, in every place on our planet. It is from here, at a fundamental philosophical level, that we must regain mastery of a normative discourse for those who find themselves at the bottom of the pile.'

François Houtart: 'What we can conclude from this discussion is that when we face the problems we are dealing with, and seek their solution, diverse values and sensibilities come into play. Each person reacts in terms of his or her own experience. Such diverse sensibilities are not exclusive, and this richness is positive. Still, it will clearly be impossible to integrate *everything* that has been said in the press conference tomorrow, and so we should be realistic and draw up an agenda of concrete proposals. We have a schedule of proposals which relate to the medium term and we have to complete these with the information gathered in discussion.

I think that this can be summarized in four main points. First, the *contents* of the work: a series of suggestions have been made and I will just give a few examples, not in any particular order. We spoke of the global dimension of social organization, of the political rather than simply the economic dimension of globalization, of the problem of refugees throughout the world, of the process of democratization, of private property, of taxation, of unemployment, of the state, of oil and its significance for the Gulf War, of the right to life, of nuclear apartheid and of many other topics. All that should be put in a certain order, so as to present it in a logical manner.

The second point is a question of *methodology*. The problem is indeed to develop a pedagogy which will allow us to move from analysis at the micro level to a macro-level understanding of the problem of economic globalization and its social effects.

The third point takes in our discussion of the type of collaboration between the different social movements, NGOs and other groups, and the different types of *alliance* which can be established for action.

The fourth point is about *mobilization*, particularly the five areas that Christophe Aguiton outlined: international treaties, debt, international institutions, regulation and the defence/conquest of democracy.

These are the main points our discussion covered. We may hope that the broad spread of ideas and proposals reflects the depth of individual involvement in the social action process over a long period of time. We can now draw certain conclusions for tomorrow, but we should also draw up a longer-term agenda. As Robert Crémiaux has said, we have to be very clear, simple and modest, but also incisive, in the way we speak. For now, please read the paper prepared by the committee: see if it represents what we want to say tomorrow, and which parts of it could serve as a basis for longer-term joint action in line with what Riccardo Petrella has said regarding different actions that can be imagined simultaneously – the many stories making up the alternative story that challenges neoliberal discourse.' (The press statement, 'For Another Davos', is on page 110.)

The Press Conference at Davos

The press conference took place on Saturday 28 January in a hotel in Davos, close to the Congress Room where the World Economic Forum was being held. Two points should be clarified. First, that we are not reproducing here the whole of the press conference but the moments we judge to be the most significant. Second, the press conference was enlarged through the presence of a giant screen linked to the Internet, thus permitting thousands of interested people to experience the event live.

François Houtart: 'I would like to remind you that the diversity of people participating in this press conference is very great, and that the unity of the group rests on the struggle against the world capitalist system and against the new strategies being discussed by the men present today at Davos. These strategies are manifold: first, a degree of regulation of financial capital to prevent the whole system from collapsing; second, the search for a new social contract, with Jean-Jacques Rousseau being hauled out of his grave to help them find new inspiration; and, finally, the use of the voluntary NGO organizations, the churches and religious people to battle against poverty. The Davos discourse carefully avoids saying that poverty is aggravated by the system itself.'

Question from a journalist: 'Have you tried to participate in the Forum and if not, why not? Second, do you believe in a form of dialogue or will it be inevitably antagonistic?

Bernard Cassen: 'No, we have absolutely *not* asked to be invited to the Forum. Doubtless we would have been had we so wished. We do not wish to play bit parts in it – as do, unfortunately, many who are there to bring a bit of spirit to a show which aims at something else, to provide a consensus of the élite (whether they be financiers, politicians or industrialists) on globalization, and on the best way to change things so as not to change anything. We have no desire to be involved in this game. But we nevertheless wanted to be present in this town in a symbolic way to hold the discussions we have had.

On the second question: of course, different forms of dialogue are always possible, but they always take place within a certain power relationship. Our project is a civil project, a citizens' project. It is to ensure that the ideas we propose, which are shared by tens of millions of people across the world (we don't know exactly how many), progress in such a way that decision makers take them into account within the terms of a new power relationship. If we simply have a modest dialogue with the men of Davos, I believe that we will be received courteously, but that has strictly no interest for us.'

Question from a journalist: 'Regarding the criticism that you formulate about the discussions there, do you have the impression that there has been a change of spirit or tone over these past two years, and particularly this past year? Do you think that this is anything more than the lowering of a façade, or is it due to the crisis which has taken place? What is your analysis of the situation?'

Samir Amin: 'There *has* been a change of tone, and it is not only a lowering of the façade. It is a fact that there is a crisis, but it is not important that the protagonists of the Davos Forum did not foresee it, whilst others did see it coming. They are confronted with new threats to their point of view. So they have opted for a word which was previously banned by them: *regulation*. But there is regulation and regulation. What they are proposing, and they will not go further than this, is regulation as carried out by themselves. That is to say, by the transnationals themselves – and perhaps by some organizations and institutions which are the instruments of transnational policies, such as the WTO, the IMF and the World Bank.

But what is totally excluded, and what the participants at the Davos International Economic Forum have not introduced into their new language, is *social regulation*. By this I mean regulation which is the result of negotiation between the antagonistic interests of the different nations, which would involve the trade unions, elected representatives and popular organizations on the one hand, and the bosses and capital on the other. This would lead to an historic compromise involving the state (not only as it is often presented in caricature style, as a gang of technocrats and stupid autocratic bureaucrats) but as an effective instrument to implement a transparent and democratic social contract. That is a form of regulation which is totally excluded in the perspective of the Davos Forum.

The only form of regulation that the latter envisages is that operated by the economic powers, in the place of deregulation, which was also a form of clandestine regulation by them, but under other conditions. In this sense, there is something other than a change of tone. There is a new challenge. But the proposals the participants of the Davos Forum are making will be insufficient. Let me give you an example. A year or two from now they could adopt a type of Tobin tax. But how do they propose to manage it? By themselves, through a consortium of large investors, by institutional formulae that they will invent? Whatever they decide, it will certainly not be to manage it through, for example, a democratic organization of the international system.'

Question from François Laborde, France 2: 'I have two questions to put to you concerning globalization and globality. Don't you make any distinction between the approaches and analyses which might be made by countries or politicians who have spoken here at the Davos Forum? Do you have the feeling that the analysis is the same, whether it is presented by the Americans or the Germans, for example? And finally, regarding the economic perspectives, we have the impression that there is much pessimism at Davos. Some speak of deflation and recession. Do you have the same type of analysis? If so, in which sector and in which country?

Bernard Cassen: 'To reply to the question of divergences of view. It is true that there are divergences, but they are situated within a broad zone of convergence. The three great "fundamental" liberties of capital are total freedom of capital movement; the freedom to invest, which the MAI cast aside for a short time; and the freedom of free trade. On these great principles – the same ones which are destroying our planet – there is total agreement. And this agreement was recalled in the December declaration of the Social Democratic ministers of finance, as represented by Dominique Strass Khann for France and Oskar Lafontaine for Germany. They all restated their attachment to these principles. Whilst divergences there may be, it is this framework that we are fighting against.'

Question from a journalist: 'You, the Other Davos, are confronted with the same underlying problem as Davos itself: the increasingly phenomenal power of technology and information. What do you propose for regulating these technologies? '

Susan George: 'I believe that there are fully positive aspects for us. I would like to take the example of the MAI. It is scarcely a year since that was proposed and nevertheless, thanks to computer technology and to contacts that we can establish rapidly across the Internet, there are coalitions in over twenty countries which worked together, which have undertaken actions together, on the same day, each one in its own country, and which were united around texts worked out jointly over the Internet. Without the development of these techniques, which are not entirely negative, we would not have achieved the result of killing off the MAI at the OECD. I was very proud when I read in the *Financial Times* that we are being called the Internet guerrillas. And they said,

"Who are these people anyway?" Well, "those people" were in fact many people, of very diverse origins and backgrounds, who had one thing in common. And that is that they saw that MAI was going to kill democracy if it was passed, and so each one got mobilized in his or her home country. Thus, there are extremely positive aspects in the new technologies for movements such as ours that we want to develop, including for the Other Davos.'

Question from a journalist: 'You were speaking of alternatives just now, but are there not some convergences with the official Davos? I have come from a debate where Romano Prodi said: "Basically, Europe is very old now and has nothing to offer its young people, it has no grand challenge to propose." Is this not something you could discuss? The president of Nestlé said, "What is important for me is education, it is essential to learn throughout one's life" – even if he added, in parallel to this, that the euro will help his enterprises relocate more easily.'

François Houtart: 'I believe that it is easy to respond to this type of proposition. A number of positions and some of the measures proposed can indeed sound identical on the lips of the defenders of the system and on those of its critics. There is a similar vocabulary, but a funda-mentally different philosophy. We are thus facing a semantic problem. We are talking about the use of a vocabulary and even about the adoption of propositions of a cultural or social type by the financial powers, in which they espouse the same terms and even the same analyses as those on the Left, whilst having a point of departure and above all a destination which are radically opposed.'

Question from a journalist: 'I agree, but if you will permit me I would like to go back to the question from my colleague. If, after all, you are using the same technologies, can you not also use some of the same concepts and effectively take radically different points of view, while the conceptual infrastructure remains the same?'

François Houtart: 'I don't believe so. I think rather that it is the content of the proposition that is different, whilst it appears similar.'

Bernard Cassen: 'I think that the Davos leaders have a great capacity for creating terminology, for creating words and for twisting words. They take words in their everyday usage and make them say something else. I too would like to quote the president of Nestlé. He made some provocative statements about the "guerrilla workers" of whom Susan George spoke, by denying them all democratic legitimacy. But what democratic legitimacy does the president of Nestlé have? He is here at the World Economic Forum as an important person, but he is also a member of the European Round Table of Industrialists and the International Chamber of Commerce. He is what in France we call a *cumulard* (a job accumulator). But when he says he is interested in education, I say, be cautious. Since you should know that the European Round Table of Industrialists supports the privatization of educational institutions in Europe. It is actually extremely dangerous when the president of Nestlé gets interested in this sector!

As for the proposal from Mr Prodi, I cannot but go along with it. Let's hear it again, is there really a project for Europe? Is the independence of the European Central Bank a project for Europe? Is the global market a great project for Europe? Will you mobilize the young people, will people man the barricades to defend the Central Bank? To defend a strong euro? We are indeed waiting for a project. We are among those who will contribute to it.'

Riccardo Petrella: 'I would like to reply quickly to the question on education. There is a difference here. Education today in the industrial environment and in the political and cultural environments consists of: how to ensure that the human resources (since both you and I are now reduced to being 'human resources' rather than human beings) can be trained on a continuing basis, throughout our lives, to be recycled at the right moment, to be a profitable human resource. That is the role given to training. This is not our objective. In fact, be careful yourself that you don't become a human resource. Because once you become a human resource, and you are no longer profitable, people will ask you what right you have to exist.'

A journalist: 'Why do you think I am here today?'

15

Manifesto:
What The Other Davos Stands For

The Other Davos was rich in meetings, contributions and resolutions. But it also had significant repercussions in the media. The outcome of these meetings between people of different origins is given form in a text entitled 'For Another Davos'. This joint statement is a tangible sign that the process of convergence is possible, one milestone amongst many for an ever-growing association of social forces and citizens engaged in a common struggle.

For Another Davos

The policies applied in recent years and initiated by the 'global leaders' present at the Davos meetings, policies defined by the GATT/WTO, by the IMF and the World Bank, have led to a distribution of resources which is inefficient, unequal, and unjust. This has led in turn to a hectic race for profits and the appropriation by a few people of most of the world's wealth, and to the devastation of the planet's ecosystem. Today these leaders recognize that they were wrong. However, they maintain that the current functioning of a capitalist market economy, free and unregulated, is the only option.

The four networks that initiated this meeting believe that the 'globalization' of resistance and struggle is imperative. Everywhere women and men are challenging the supposed inevitability of the present system. Building alternatives is possible today, on the basis of their experiences and creativity.

Faced by the challenges with which the globalization of capital confronts us, we are encouraged and strengthened by the sources of resistance and social movements that we represent and with which we are in solidarity. We shall coordinate our efforts and increase the pressures we bring to bear on the system in different domains.

Commerce and investment. Building on our initial victory over the MAI, we oppose the plan to transfer an almost unchanged text to the WTO or the Transatlantic Economic Partnership, and to the 'Millennium Round' of the WTO. All these plans are based on the subordination of political power to transnational capital.

International financial system. We demand cancellation of the debt of all countries of the Third World and of Central and Eastern Europe. The international financial system and its institutions should be completely overturned and subordinated to political democracy. The 'independence' of central banks is unacceptable. We demand the elimination of tax havens, and the application of taxes on financial transactions, for example the 'Tobin tax'.

Development. We must break with the destructive structural adjustment policies of the international financial institutions such as the IMF, the World Bank, and the London and Paris clubs, and rethink and reconstitute a new international financial system based on a fair allocation of resources for the basic needs of peoples, based on justice and freedom.

Peace and security. The overall policy of double standards in international relationships is unacceptable, whether in international law or in the application of United Nations resolutions, or in embargoes imposed on peoples. The system of the United Nations must be democratized.

Rights and liberties. These demands cannot be separated from the guarantee of civil, trade union and political rights, nor from equal rights between women and men, as well as the extension of individual and collective rights to the social, economic and ecological domains, as proposed in the United Nations Universal Declaration of Human Rights.

We propose many alternatives at different levels. They are rooted in social needs and the fair allocation of wealth produced by work. Their aim is to re-embed the economy in society, and to safeguard the future of the biosphere. The principles of social economy, agrarian reforms, collective rights of citizens and workers, freedom to travel and to settle, systems of social protection and of public and civic responsibility must prevail. We also demand that health and educational institutions be improved and adapted, that spending on armaments be reduced, and that these industries be converted for civilian use.

To those who speak of the 'invisible hand' of the market, we stress the hands and the intelligence of women and men. These hands and these minds are building today's economy, which generations to come will inherit. Against the oppression and arrogance of the powerful, the outlines of a new world are being drawn. In this world, citizens and workers will decide on the distribution of wealth and the organization of work. They will be in charge of the future.

16

A SUMMARY OF THE PROCESS

FRANÇOIS HOUTART

The World Economic Forum met in Davos at the end of January and simultaneously some sixty people met in Zürich (27–31 January 1999), at the invitation of four organizations: ATTAC (Association for the Taxation of Financial Transactions in the Interests of the Citizen), the Coalition against MAI, the World Forum for Alternatives and SAPRIN (Structural Adjustment Participatory Review International Network). Five social movements were also invited to take part in this meeting. They were MST (Movement of Landless Farmworkers) from Brazil, PICIS (Policy and Information Centre for International Solidarity) from South Korea, FENOP (National Federation of Farmers' Organizations) from Burkina Faso, the Women's Movement from Quebec and the Movement of the Unemployed from France.

Several analysts of international repute were also present, including Samir Amin, Riccardo Petrella, Susan George, François Chesnais and Charles-André Udry. Over twenty nationalities were represented from all the continents of the world.

Preceding the press conference in Davos a conference lasting one and a half days was held in Zürich, and on the agenda were four main points:

- a critique of the current world economic order;

- alternatives to be proposed;

- the links between social movements working at grassroots level and centres of research and analysis;

- the future organization of international cooperation between social movements and centres of research and analysis at the global level.

At the end of the meeting a manifesto was issued (see p. 111), and a calendar of planned activities was drawn up, including certain initiatives which the organizers of The Other Davos will take forward.

113

All participants were able to make helpful contacts, define their medium- and long-term objectives, and plan possible future cooperation.

On Saturday 30 January a press conference was held in Davos in a hotel situated 300 metres from the place where the World Economic Forum was being held. Some thirty journalists as well as Swiss television were present at the press conference. The Forum in Davos exercised a tight monopoly on the means of communication, making our task difficult.

Bernard Cassen of *Le Monde Diplomatique* opened the press conference, with François Houtart in the chair. Samir Amin explained why this alternative Davos was taking place, Susan George presented the organizers and the movements involved, and Riccardo Petrella spoke about the significance of the intervention and its future. After the conference individual interviews were given either on site or by telephone with newspapers or periodicals in Europe, America and the Middle East.

The following day, a further meeting was held, involving the organizers and the social movements. This meeting looked at the question of continuity, as this was the main objective: the press conference was an opportunity which could not be passed up, but it was not the main aim of the meeting.

The first joint activity was set for June 1999 in Paris, bringing together several hundred people to discuss the theme of the omnipresence of financial capital and its controlling power – the unifying theme of the initiatives indicated in the calendar of events.

At the same time as the meetings were being held in Zürich and Davos, several public demonstrations had been organized in Paris, Brussels and Milan to draw attention to the predominance of financial capital within the phenomenon of globalization. These meetings were organized within the framework of the Zürich and Davos meetings.

An Internet site was set up at the beginning of January. Over the course of the three weeks preceding the Zürich and Davos meetings, 228,000 consultations were made and nearly 110,000 pages were printed in over 60 countries. During the press conference, a screen carried continuous communication with many people from all over the world, all of whom had taken part in the event via the Internet site.

Thus The Other Davos had an extremely positive outcome.

1   The press conference was covered by several international papers and was the main story on Swiss television on 30 January. Media repercussions continued to be felt in succeeding months as a carefully prepared press dossier enabled journalists to draw on various lively and informative documents.

2 This first coordination of very diverse networks was in itself positive. The participants were able to maintain their own identities and objectives while managing to agree on common action in terms of focus, organizational aspects and access to the media.

3 The experience of a task undertaken on the basis of collaboration between the grassroots movements and centres of research and analysis proved very fruitful. It also showed the need to develop a specific method for this type of contact that respects local needs while developing an analytical and global perspective.

4 The importance of continuity of action became clear: different initiatives should not be one-off events but feed into the accumulation of knowledge, experience and analysis, becoming part of a long-term dynamic.

PART IV

CONCLUSION
The Time Has Come to Reclaim the March of History

THE GLOBAL FORUM FOR ALTERNATIVES

By way of conclusion, we reproduce the manifesto of the World Forum for Alternatives, adopted in Cairo in March 1997, to express the spirit and the objectives of The Other Davos.

It Is Time to Reclaim the March of History

Humanity's future is at stake. Scientific progress and technical advances, the supreme achievements of knowledge, fortify the privilege and comfort of a minority. Instead of contributing to the well-being of all, these feats are used to crush, marginalize and exclude countless human beings. Access to natural resources, especially in the South, is monopolized by the few and is subject to political blackmail and threats of war. *It is time to reclaim the march of history.*

It Is Time to Make the Economy Serve the Peoples of the World

The economy provides goods and services mainly to a minority. In its contemporary form, it forces the majority of the human race into strategies for abject survival, denying tens of millions of people even the right to live. The logic of neoliberal capitalism entrenches and accentuates grotesque inequalities. Propelled by faith in the market's self-regulating virtue, it reinforces the economic power of the rich and exponentially increases the number of the poor. *It is time to make the economy serve the peoples of the world.*

It Is Time to Break Down the Wall between North and South

Monopolies of knowledge, scientific research, advanced production, credit and information, all guaranteed by international institutions,

117

create a relentless polarization both at the global level and within each country. Trapped in patterns of development that are culturally destructive, physically unsustainable and economically submissive, many people throughout the world can neither define for themselves the stages of their evolution, establish the basis of their own growth, or provide education for their younger generations. *It is time to break down the wall between North and South.*

It Is Time to Confront the Crisis of Our Civilization

The confines of individualism, the closed world of consumption, the supremacy of productivism and, for many, an obsessive struggle for sheer daily survival obscure humanity's larger objectives: the right to live liberated from oppression and exploitation, the right to equal opportunities, social justice, peace, spiritual fulfilment and solidarity. *It is time to confront the crisis of our civilization.*

It Is Time to Refuse the Dictatorship of Money

The concentration of economic power in the hands of transnational corporations weakens, even dismantles, the sovereignty of states. It threatens democracy – within single countries and on the global scale. The dominance of financial capital does more than imperil the world's monetary equilibrium. It transforms states into mafias. It proliferates the hidden sources of capitalist accumulation: drug trafficking, the arms trade, child slavery. *It is time to refuse the dictatorship of money.*

It Is Time to Replace Cynicism with Hope

Stock prices soar when workers are laid off. A competitive edge is gained when mass consumerdom is replaced with élite niche markets. Macro-economic indicators react positively as the ranks of the poor multiply. International economic institutions coax and compel governments to pursue structural adjustment, widening the chasm between classes and provoking mounting social conflict. International humanitarian aid trickles to those reduced to despair. *It is time to replace cynicism with hope.*

It Is Time to Rebuild and Democratize the State

The programme of dismantling the state, reducing its functions, pilfering its resources and launching sweeping privatizations leads to a demoralized public sector, weakened systems of education and health, and the eventual usurping of the state by private economic interests. Neoliberal globalization divorces the state from the population and encourages corruption and organized venality on an unprecedented scale. The state becomes a repressive instrument policing the privilege of the few. *It is time to rebuild and democratize the state.*

It Is Time to Recreate the Citizenry

Millions of people are deprived of voting rights because they are immigrants. Millions more fail to vote because they are angry or discouraged, because parties are in crisis, or because they feel impotent and excluded from political life. Elections are often distorted by influence-mongering and deceit. But democracy is about more than elections. Democracy means participation at every level of economic, political and cultural life. *It is time to recreate the citizenry.*

It Is Time to Salvage Collective Values

Modernity, conveyed by capitalism and ideologized by neoliberalism, has destroyed or profoundly corrupted existing cultures. It has imploded solidarities and dismantled convictions, extolling instead the high-performance individual evaluated on the basis of economic success. Rather than bringing emancipation to the peoples of the world, modernity is generating a crisis in education, fuelling social violence and triggering an explosion of insular movements that seek salvation and protection in nationalist, ethnic or religious identity politics. *It is time to salvage collective values.*

It Is Time to Globalize Social Struggles

In all this, it is not the internationalization of the economy *per se* that is to blame. It could represent a dramatic step forward for material, social and cultural exchanges between human beings. But in its neoliberal form it becomes a nightmare lived by the victims of unemployment, young people anxious about the future, workers shut out of the productive system and nations subjected to structural adjustment, labour deregulation, the erosion of social security systems and the elimination of networks serving the poor. It purports to link and unite, yet separates and imprisons. *It is time to globalize social struggles.*

It Is Time to Build on People's Resistance

Across the world, people are organizing resistance, engaging in social struggles and creating alternatives. Women, men, children, unemployed people, excluded and oppressed people, workers, landless peasants, communities suffering from racism, impoverished city dwellers, indigenous peoples, students, intellectuals, migrants, small business people, outcasts, declining middle classes – *citizens* – are asserting their dignity, demanding respect for their human rights and natural heritages, and practising solidarity. Some have given their lives for these causes. Others practise heroism in their day-to-day existences. Some are rebuilding knowledge on the basis of experiences of struggle, some are trying out new economic forms, some are creating the basis of a new kind of politics, and some are inventing new cultures. *It is time to build on people's resistance.*

Now Is the Time for Joining Forces

We are seeing a convergence of struggles, of knowledge, of resistances, of innovations, of minds and hearts for a world of justice and equality, invention and material progress, optimism and spiritual development. We can build this world by seeking and discovering viable alternatives to neoliberalism and unilateral globalization, alternatives based on the interests of peoples and respect for national, cultural and religious differences. *Now is the time for joining forces.*

A Time for Creative Universal Thought Has Arrived

Honest, probing analysis of the current economic organization and its economic, social, ecological, political and cultural consequences can only delegitimize this phenomenon, which is paraded to the world as the paragon of progress. The search for a balance between personal initiative and the pursuit of collective goals – based on a celebration of human diversity and creativity – must open the way to new models. Studies of expanding non-market sectors, productive techniques that respect the well-being of those who use them, and the organization and nature of work will help create more human forms of organization. *A time for creative universal thought has arrived.*

The Time to Rebuild and Extend Democracy Is Here

Democracy is no longer merely a goal for the organization of societies. It is also the key to the functioning of communities, social movements, political parties, businesses, institutions, nations and international bodies. It is the means of respecting popular interests, and thus of preserving national and international security. By prising open spaces for all cultures – not patronizingly, but because they represent humanity's endowment – we can reverse the retreat into enclaves of narrow self-interest and the seclusion of identity politics. The existence of democratic, competent and transparent states is the basis of restoring their power to regulate. Regional economics and political groupings based on international complementarity are viable answers to the real needs of the global population and a necessary alternative to neoliberal globalization. Strengthening and democratizing regional and inter-national institutions is a realistic imperative. It is a condition for progress in international law and the indispensable regulation of economic, social and political relations at the global level, particularly in the fields of financial capital, taxation, migration, information and disarmament. *The time to rebuild and extend democracy is here.*

POSTSCRIPT
Porto Alegre Call for Mobilization
January 2001
The World Social Forum

Social forces from around the world have gathered here at the World Social Forum in Porto Alegre. Unions and NGOs, movements and organizations, intellectuals and artists, together we are building a great alliance to create a new society, resisting the dominant logic in which the free market and money are considered the only measure of worth. Davos represents the concentration of wealth, the globalization of poverty and the destruction of our earth. Porto Alegre represents the hope that a new world is possible, where human beings and nature are the centre of our concern. We are part of a movement which has grown since Seattle. We challenge the élite and their undemocratic processes, symbolized by the World Economic Forum in Davos. We came here to share our experiences, build our solidarity, and demonstrate our total rejection of the neoliberal policies of globalization.

We are women and men, farmers, workers, unemployed, professionals, students, blacks and indigenous peoples, coming from the South and from the North, committed to struggle for peoples' rights, freedom, security, employment and education. We are fighting against the hegemony of finance, the destruction of our cultures, the monopolization of knowledge, mass media, and communication, the degradation of nature, and the destruction of the quality of life by transnational corporations and anti-democratic policies. Participative democratic experiences – like that of Porto Alegre – show us that a concrete alternative is possible. We reaffirm the supremacy of human, ecological and social rights over the demands of finance and investors.

At the same time that we strengthen our movements, we resist the global élite and work for equity, social justice, democracy and security for everyone, without distinction. Our methodology and alternatives stand in stark contrast to the destructive policies of neoliberalism. Globalization reinforces a sexist and patriarchal system. It increases the feminization of poverty and exacerbates all forms of violence against women. Equality between women and men is central to our struggle. Without this, another world will never be possible.

Neoliberal globalization increases racism, continuing the veritable genocide of centuries of slavery and colonialism which destroyed the bases of black African civilizations. We call on all movements to be in solidarity with African peoples in the continent and outside, in defence of their rights to land, citizenship, freedom, peace, and equality, through the reparation of historical and social debts. The slave trade and slavery are crimes against humanity.

We express our special recognition and solidarity with indigenous peoples in their historic struggle against genocide and ethnocide and in defence of their rights, natural resources, culture, autonomy, land, and territory.

Neoliberal globalization destroys the environment, health and people's living environment. Air, water, land and peoples have become commodities. Life and health must be recognized as fundamental rights which must not be subordinated to economic policies.

The external debt of the countries of the South has been repaid several times over. Illegitimate, unjust and fraudulent, it functions as an instrument of domination, depriving people of their fundamental human rights with the sole aim of increasing international usury. We demand its unconditional cancellation and the reparation of historical, social, and ecological debts, as immediate steps toward a definitive resolution of the crisis this debt provokes.

Financial markets extract resources and wealth from communities and nations, and subject national economies to the whims of speculators. We call for the closure of tax havens and the introduction of taxes on financial transactions.

Privatization is a mechanism for transferring public wealth and natural resources to the private sector. We oppose all forms of privatization of natural resources and public services. We call for the protection of access to resources and public goods necessary for a decent life.

Transnational corporations organize global production with massive unemployment, low wages and unqualified labour, and by refusing to recognize the fundamental workers' rights as defined by the ILO. We demand the genuine recognition of the right to organize and negotiate for unions, and new rights for workers to face the globalization strategy. While goods and money are free to cross borders, the restrictions on the movement of people exacerbate exploitation and repression. We demand an end to such restrictions.

We call for a trading system which guarantees full employment, food security, fair terms of trade and local prosperity. Free trade is anything but free. Global trade rules ensure the accelerated accumulation of wealth and power by transnational corporations and the further marginalization and impoverishment of small farmers, workers and local enterprises. We demand that governments respect their obligations to the international human rights instruments and multilateral environmental agreements. We call on people everywhere to support the mobilizations against the creation of the Free Trade Area of the Americas, an initiative which means the recolonization of Latin America and the destruction of fundamental social, economic, cultural and environmental human rights.

The IMF, the World Bank and regional banks, the WTO, and NATO and other military alliances are some of the multilateral agents of neoliberal globalization. We call for an end to their interference in national policy. These institutions have no legitimacy in the eyes of the people and we will continue to protest against their measures.

Neoliberal globalization has led to the concentration of land ownership and favoured corporate agricultural systems which are environmentally and socially destructive. It is based on export-oriented growth backed by large-scale infrastructure development, such as dams, which displaces people from their land and destroys their livelihoods. Their loss must be restored. We call for a democratic agrarian reform. Land, water and seeds must be in the hands of the peasants. We promote sustainable agricultural processes. Seeds and genetic stocks are the heritage of humanity. We demand that the use of transgenics and the patenting of life be outlawed.

Militarism and corporate globalization reinforce each other to undermine democracy and peace. We totally refuse war as a way to solve conflicts and we oppose the arms race and the arms trade. We call for an end to the repression and criminalization of social protest. We condemn foreign military intervention in the internal affairs of our countries. We demand the lifting of embargoes and sanctions used as instruments of aggression, and express our solidarity with those who suffer their consequences. We reject US military intervention in Latin America through the Plan Colombia.

We call for a strengthening of alliances, and the implementation of common actions on these principal concerns. We will continue to mobilize on them until the next Forum. We recognize that we are now in a better position to undertake the struggle for a different world, a world without misery, hunger, discrimination and violence, with quality of life, equity, respect and peace.

We commit ourselves to supporting all the struggles of our common agenda to mobilize opposition to neoliberalism. Among our priorities for the coming months, we will mobilize globally against the World Economic Forum at Cancun, Mexico, on 26 and 27 February 2001; the

Free Trade Area of the Americas in Buenos Aires, 6–7 April and in Quebec City, 17–22 April; the Asian Development Bank in Honolulu, in May; the G8 Summit in Genoa, 15–22 July; the IMF and World Bank Annual Meeting in Washington, 28 September–4 October; and the World Trade Organization, 5–9 November (in Qatar?).

On 17 April 2001, we will support the international day of struggle against the importation of cheap agricultural products which create economic and social dumping, and the feminist mobilization against globalization in Genoa. We support the call for a world day of action against debt, to take place this year on 20 July.

The proposals formulated are part of the alternatives being elaborated by social movements around the world. They are based on the principle that human beings and life are not commodities, and on a commitment to the welfare and human rights of all.

Our involvement in the World Social Forum has enriched understanding of each of our struggles and we have been strengthened. We call on all peoples around the world to join in this struggle to build a better future. The World Social Forum of Porto Alegre is a way to achieve people's sovereignty and a just world.

Hundreds of organizations have signed this call. If you want to see the endorsements, please check:
http://attac.org/fra/asso/doc/doc502sign.htm

If your organization wants to sign it, please send an e-mail to attacint@attac.org, mentioning your endorsement and giving any useful information.

INDEX

AC 91
accountability 14-15
Adam Smith Institute 12
advertising 73
Afghanistan 23
Africa 38-9, 49, 53, 60-2, 66, 72, 83, 99, 123; Central 21-2; sub-Saharan 41; West 82, 86-7, 89
age 15, 64
Agir Contre le Chômage 81
agriculture *ix*, 5, 36, 39, 53, 56, 58, 61, 65, 74, 77-8, 82-3, 86-90, 95-7, 120, 122, 124-5
Aguiton, Christophe 25, 80-1, 94-8, 100-1, 104
aid 27, 41, 55, 118
Alaska 95
alienation *x*, 13
alliance politics 53-5, 58, 89, 104, 120, 122, 124
Alternatives Economiques 81
Alternatives Sud 47, 55, 83
Amara, Jean-Claude 81
Amin, Samir 18, 60, 80, 82, 98-9, 106, 113-14
Amnesty International 64-5
Amsterdam 92
APES 91
Arab Congress 81
Arab countries 60-2, 81
Argentina 40, 65, 72, 126
Asia 8, 26, 34, 38-9, 46, 52, 66, 77, 83-4, 95, 99; Central 23; East 26, 99; South 99; South-east 21, 24, 32, 40, 60, 72, 99; West 99
Asian Development Bank 126
Asian Dragons 32, 72
Asian Tigers 72, 77, 84
Asia–Pacific Economic Cooperation Forum (APEC) 60
Asile 100-1
ASPIR 100
Association for the Taxation of Financial Transactions in the Interests of the Citizen (ATTAC) 25, 32-3, 45-6, 66, 69, 71, 74, 80-1, 92, 94-7, 113
Association of South-east Asian Nations (ASEAN) 52
Australia 60

banks, central 20, 28, 66, 111; at Davos summit 82, 86; eco-banks 65; in emerging countries 34; employees' role in reforming 71; and financial crises 15, 34; industrial 26; international 26; legal regulation of 71; London Club 27; and money laundering 28; neo-mutual 65; 'new bank' 66; regional 124
Barcelona 30
Beaudet, Pierre 18

Belgium 33, 52, 83, 89
Ben Bella, Ahmed 81, 84-6
Berlin wall 48
Bertrand, Agnès 81-2
biodiversity 6
biotechnology 65; *see also* genetic engineering
British Child Poverty Action Group 11
bonds 26, 30, 40
Brazil 26, 32-3, 40, 46, 48, 61, 65, 72, 82, 85, 89-90, 95, 97, 100, 102, 113
Bretton Woods system 7, 66, *see also* IMF, international financial institutions, World Bank
British Aerospace 12
British Telecom 12
Brittan, Sir Leon 99
Brussels 114
Buenos Aires 126
bureaucracy 19, 27, 48, 56, 102, 106
Burkina Faso 78, 82, 86-9

CACES 55
Cairo 117
Canada 126
Cancun 124
capital flows 20, 26, 34-6, 38, 107
capitalism, alliance capitalism 10; alternatives to 18, 35, 43, 47-60; crisis of 19, 26, 35-6, 59, 118; cycle of production 36-7; and development 50; evolution of 94-5; global 3, 30, 50-1, 53, 63-4, 66, 99, 102, 105; 'Great Mass' at Davos 86; injustice generated by 3; logic of *ix*, 17, 68-9, 78, 117; oligopolistic 19-21; post-capitalism *ix*; precapitalist social relations 49; and profit motive *xi*, 11, 18, *see also* profit; and public sector 11-13; 'real' 47-9; reproduction of 48; restructuring of 72; ruling class 17; and society 48, 50; system 50-2; and technology 48; and worker democracy 55; worker organization under 48; *see also* finance capital, neoliberalism
Cassen, Bernard 105, 107-9, 114
Catholic University of Louvain 83
Central America 48, 72
Central Intelligence Agency (CIA) 23, 86
CGT/Committee of the Unemployed 91
Chesnais, François 32, 81, 103, 113
Chiapas 49, 58, 65
Chicago 30, 85
Chicago, University of 9
children 5, 11, 66, 73, 90, 118, 120; International Convention on the Rights of the Child (1989) 64

126

Chile 65
China 10, 13, 21-2, 40, 60-1, 85
Churches 97, 100-1, 105
citizenship, and activism 69; in Africa 123;
and consumerdom *xi*; and debt
cancellation 72; and democracy 20, 119;
and dialogue 105; and education 68;
farmers as 83; and financial system 69, 71;
and globalization of social struggles 120;
and incomes 64; and the MAI 14; and
market dictatorship 46; and the media 68;
protection of 7; recreation of 119; rights of
70, 111-12; and social movements 77;
solidarity of 72; sovereignty of 67
civil society *viii*, 55, 66
class, comprador 54; cross-border bases of 51;
dominant 35-6, 60; exploitation 78;
middle 13, 53-4; new world oligarchy 31;
ruling 17, 98, 100; working 18, 53-4, 61
Coalition against the MAI 16, 72-3, 80-2, 92,
95, 99-100, 107-8, 113
Cohen-Hadria, Victor 80, 84-5
Cold War 27
Cologne 92, 98
colonialism 48, 123; decolonization 8, 27;
neocolonialism 82
Comité des Sans-Logis 91
Committee for the Cancellation of Third
World Debt (CADTM) 38-9
commoditization 28
common good 101-3
Commonwealth of Independent States (CIS)
5; *see also* Russia, Soviet Union
communism 36
community life *xi*, 64
comparative advantage 21
competition 10-11, 15, 30, 33, 50, 68, 98
Confédération Paysanne 91
conflict 21, 25, 29, 60, 84, 118, 124
consumerism *xi*, 11-12, 28, 36-7, 47, 58, 71, 118
cooperatives 28, 54, 56, 86-90
Copenhagen 30
corruption 28, 34, 93-4, 119
Crémieux, Robert 90-2, 104
culture *viii*, *ix*, 20, 27-9, 31, 50-1, 56-8, 78-9,
118-21, 122-4

Dakar 52
DAL 91
debt, on agenda of social action 104; and aid
41; blackmailing of poor countries on 38;
cancellation of 38-41, 46, 65-6, 71-4, 96-7,
111, 123, 126; crises 14, 34, 38, 40, 74, 123;
and development 6; increasing 85;
irrecoverable 26; and living standards 6;
and neoliberalism 19; reduction of 57;
repayment of 41; rescheduling of 73;
servicing of 70, 85; 'social and ecological'
71; and social welfare spending 6, 70;
solidarity on 72; and state 34; and
structural adjustment 39-41; US 41
decentralization 55, 87
democracy, on agenda of social action 104;
and agrarian reform 124; and alternatives

to capitalism 48; and citizenship 119; as
common capital of humanity 103; and
current crisis 60; and decolonization 27;
defence of 97, 102-4; degradation of 20-1;
and dialogue *x*, 105; electoral 20, 52, 54-5,
102, 119; exclusion from 119; and
financial system *ix*, 14-16, 54, 69, 71, 111,
118; and globalization 20, 67, 118, 121;
illusion of 60; and law 19; and legitimacy
31, 108-9; low-intensity 20; and the MAI
108; and market system 18, 20-1, 26; and
migrants 119; and military 124; and
neoliberalism 23, 54-5; participatory *ix*,
119, 122; popular pressure for 52; and
quality of life 122; rebuilding 120-1;
reconquest of 103; rethinking beyond
multi-partyism 54-5; right to 64; and
social contract 106-7; as social movement
61; and solidarity 31; and state 19, 54-5,
118, 121; and transnational coporations
118; and United Nations 58, 111; and
workers 55; and world parliament 102
deregulation 4, 14, 17-18, 28, 30, 35-7, 49, 53-4,
69-70, 78, 93-4, 97, 106, 119; *see also*
liberalization
Detroit 30
devaluation 19, 87
development, agencies 88-9; and agriculture
83, 88-9; and Bretton Woods institutions
7; and capitalism 50; crisis of 84; and
culture 86-9, 118; and energy
consumption 6; and globalization 32, 62;
inequality of 19-20, 29, 111, 118; and
poverty 5; and structural adjustment 111;
sustainable 53, 68, 70-1, 118; and trade 13;
Triad controls 98-9; and underdevelopment 70
Development GAP 81
disarmament 39, 121; *see also* nuclear power
and trade, arms
Disney, Walt 50
Drois Devants (Rights First) 82, 91
drugs 28, 73, 118
dumping 126

Eastern bloc 48, 54
eco-development *see* sustainability
ecology *see* environment
economic growth 4-5, 6, 21, 32, 118, 124
education 4-6, 16, 41, 64-5, 67-8, 70, 73, 90,
108-9, 111, 118-19, 122
electricity 11, 67
Elf 98
employment 5, 12, 28, 31, 36, 65-6, 123; job
creation 5, 10, 14, 70
energy 6, 84, 90
Entraide et Fraternité 89
environment, and agriculture 83, 90, 124;
defence of *ix*; destruction of *viii*, 122;
economic analysis of 79; and economic
growth 29, 84; ecosystem 29, 63, 65, 110;
and human rights 64, 111; and market
system 8-9; movements *ix*, 61, 77;
multilateral agreements on 124; and

128 INDEX

of *ix*; regeneration of 16; regulation of 57-
8; as social cost 29; struggle for 64;
sustainability of 53; and technology 90
equality 74, 120, 123 120
Espagne, Vincent 82
ethics 58
ethnicity 22, 29, 49, 54, 78, 119; ethnic
cleansing 22
Europe 8, 11, 28, 32, 34, 39, 46, 61-2, 67, 69-70,
72-3, 81, 91-2, 94, 101, 108-9, 114; Central
5, 111; Eastern 5, 19, 40, 51, 95, 111;
Northern 97
European Central Bank 109
European Marches against Unemployment,
Employment Insecurity and Exclusion 81,
91-2, 94
European Round Table of Industrialists 109
European Trade Union Confederation 95
European Union (EU) 32, 34, 52, 60, 70, 83, 87,
102
exchange control 21-2
exchange rate 25, 33, 66
exclusion *xi*, 9, 15, 17-18, 36, 81, 94, 117, 119-
20
exports 32-3, 38, 85-6, 124

famine 36
Federation of Cooperative Farmers of
Burkina Faso (FENOP) 78, 86-9
Federation of Korean Trade Unions (FKTU)
93
finance capital, and agriculture 83; and crime
33; and culture 33; and democracy *ix*, 14-
16, 54, 69, 71, 111, 118; and development
agencies 88-9; domination of 28, 31, 33,
51, 114; as global system 99; and
globalization 21, 32-7, 69, 99, 114;
hegemony of 122; market 14-15, 19-22, 28,
32, 34, 36, 40, 69-70, 85, 93-5, 118; and
'other globalization' strategies 66-7; and
pension funds 28, 33, 36, 70-1, 97; and
politics 33; reform of 69; regulation of 35,
71, 74, 77, 121; and social welfare 65; and
society 33; and state 118; and taxation 15,
33, 39, 46, 57, 70-1, 74, 77, 97, 106-7, 111,
123
Financial Times 107
financial crises, Asian (1997) 8, 21-2, 26, 32,
34, 40, 84; Brazilian 95; and capital
accumulation 35-6; complexity of 34;
contagion effect of 34; Crash (of 1929) 37;
Crash (of 1987) 32; current 5, 8-9, 19-21,
35-6, 70, 77, 95-6; European currency
crisis (1991–2) 32; and exclusion 36; and
globalization 34; and inequality 14, 19;
Japanese 26, 32, 95; Korean 21, 95; Latin
American 26, 32, 40; Mexican (1994) 21,
26, 32; and neoliberalism 9, 19; and
overproduction 35-6; and privatization
34; Russian (1998) 5, 8, 21-2, 26, 32, 34;
structural 19-21
financial speculation 14-15, 21, 33-5, 41, 57,
69-71, 74, 77, 85, 97, 123

Food and Agriculture Organization (FAO) 27,
64
food security 4, 64, 70, 73, 85, 102, 123
Forum of the Small Villages of the World 83
Forum of the Third World 82
France 2, 17, 21, 68, 72, 78, 81, 86, 88, 90-2, 99,
107, 113
Frankfurt 30
Free Trade Area of the Americas 124-5
Friedman, Milton 9
FSU 91

G22 countries 73
G7 countries 22-4, 39, 73-4, 99; Counter-G7 98
G8 countries 126
gas 11, 67
General Agreement on Tariffs and Trade
(GATT) 66, 110
genetic engineering 95, 102, 124
genocide *viii*, 123
Genoa 126
George, Susan 80, 82, 99-100, 102, 107-8, 113-14
Germany 9, 21, 107
globalization, and agricture 82; alternative
x, 52, 61, 75; and capitalist system 3, 30,
50-1, 53, 63-4, 66, 99, 102, 105; of
consumer markets 28; of culture 77; and
democracy 20; and development 32; and
finance capital 21, 32-7, 69, 99, 114; and
financial crises 34; life appropriated by
31; and media 70; national perspectives of
107; and neocolonialism 82; and
neoliberalism 20-3, 73; political 21, 29-30;
popular resistance to 52; redefinition of
52; regulation of 35; sham 29-30; social
consequences of 77; social forces of 110; of
social struggles 60-2, 119-20; and
sovereignty 32; and state 30, 32, 67, 118-
19; of trade 29; and unemployment 119
Gorbachev, Mikhail 27
Gore, Al 60
Gramsci, Antonio 9
grassroots 9, 54, 79, 113, 115
Great Depression (1930s) 4, 37
Greenpeace 64
Groupe de Lisbonne 83
Gulf states 22
Gulf War (1991) 22, 96, 104

Haiti 55
Hayek, Friedrich von 9-10, 17
health 4-6, 15-16, 36, 41, 64, 67, 70, 73, 85, 90,
111, 119, 123
hedge funds 28
hegemony *ix*, 9, 20, 79, 82, 98, 122
Hellinger, Douglas 80-1
Heritage Foundation 13
history 17, 26, 31, 52, 56, 59-60, 117
homelessness 36, 64-5, 82, 90, 97, 100
Hong Kong 30
Honolulu 126
housing *see* homelessness
Houston 30
Houtart, François 18, 47, 77, 80, 83, 94, 103-5,

130 INDEX

Movement of the Unemployed 78, 81, 90-2, 97, 113
Mozambique 6
Multilateral Agreement on Investment (MAI) 14, 16, 19, 39, 45-6, 65-6, 70, 72-3, 77, 80-2, 92, 95-6, 99-100, 107-8, 111, 113
Munich 30

Nagoya 30
nationalism *viii*, 119
natural resources 6, 53, 57-8, 117, 123
neoliberalism, alternatives to *ix-x*, 16, 47-60; and capitalist system 3; and civil society 55; and competition 10-11; consensus challenged 43; counter-offensive begins 45-6; and culture 50, 56; and debt 19; delegitimizing 50; and democracy 14-15, 54-5; discourse of 104; effects of 4; and environment 8-9, 123; ethical critique of 50; and exclusion 9, 15, 18; failure to function as human economy 50; and financial crises 9, 19; and globalization 20-3, 73; history of 7-16; ideological offensive of 9; and inequality 13-15, 19; and international financial organizations *viii*; and landless farmers 89; limits of its system 85; logic of 78, 117; as minority view post-war 8; as 'natural' 9, 16; as 'new world order' 21, 26; and NGOs 55; optimistic faith in market 35-6, 49; and politics 15; and privatization 11-13; and redistribution of wealth 13-15; as religion 9; social relations not considered by 49; and state 28, 118-19; and structural adjustment 14, 72, 94; as total liberalism 17; and transparency 14-15; triumph of 9; winners and losers under 15-16
Nestlé 108-9
networking *xi*, 9, 18, 30, 33, 46, 65, 69, 77-9, 96-8, 110, 115, 119
New Deal 8
New York 30, 40
Nicaragua 56, 86
Nigeria 38
Nixon, Richard 13
non-governmental organizations (NGOs) 24, 55-6, 78-9, 81, 91, 96-7, 104-5, 122
North American Free Trade Agreement (NAFTA) 70
North Atlantic Treaty Organization (NATO) 124
North–South relations *x*, *xi*, 5, 16, 57, 70, 81, 84-5, 94, 117-18
nuclear power 23, 68, 104

Observatoire de la mondialisation 81-2
Oceania 83
oil 22-3, 104
Olympic Games 29
Operation Desert Fox 22
Organization for Economic Cooperation and Development (OECD) 5, 6, 26, 36, 70, 99, 107
Osaka 30

Oslo accord 22
Ouedraogo, Ousséni 82, 86-9
overproduction 33, 35-6
Oxfam 64

panchayats 55
pandemics 36
Papart, Jean-Pierre 86
Paris 30, 114
Paris Club 111
patents 30, 95, 124; on life 95, 124
peace movement 68
pedagogy of the possible, 100, 104
pension funds 28, 33, 36, 70-1, 97
People's Power for the Twenty-first century (PP XXI) 52, 77
Permanent People's Tribunal 98
Peru 65
Petrella, Riccardo 25, 83, 101-4, 109, 113-14
Phillips, Kevin 13
Pinochet, General 65
Plan Colombia 124
Plihon, Dominique 32
pluralism 61
Poahan 93
Polanyi, Karl 8
Policy and Information Centre for International Solidarity (PICIS) 92-4, 113
pollution 6, 29, 53, 58
polycentrism 53
population 5-6, 38, 64, 85
Porto Alegre meeting (1997) 52; (2001) *viii*, *x*, 122-5
postmodernism 51-2
poverty, and aid 55; feminization of *ix*, 6, 49, 122; and financial speculation 97; globalization of 84, 92, 122; growth of 4-5, 13-14, 50, 69, 117-19; line 5, 10; in midst of plenty 8, 85, 90; and neoliberalism 18, 77, 105; networks of support 119; and NGOs 55; as social movement 77; statistics on 3-6; and Third World debt 38; urban 120; World Bank's 'struggle against' 24
power 7, 43, 48-9, 52-6, 58, 105
Primakov, Evgeni 22
privatization *viii*, *ix*, 4, 11-13, 28, 30, 40, 49, 67-8, 70, 78, 93, 103, 109, 118-19, 123
Prodi, Romano 108-9
productivism 118
profit *viii*, *x*, 11, 14, 18, 19, 31, 64, 70, 77, 94, 110
progress 29
property 21, 25, 34, 67, 102-4; *see also* intellectual property rights
protectionism 39
public relations 9, 12
public sector 6, 11-13, 67; *see also* state

Qatar 126
Quebec 33, 78, 113, 126
Quebec City 126

racism 39, 77, 120, 122-3
railway services 11

ZED TITLES ON GLOBALIZATION

The ongoing headlong rush towards an economically much more integrated world – which is usually referred to as globalization – is intimately connected to the changing nature of capitalism, and to one strand of economic theory and policy which is currently dominant – neoliberalism. Zed Books has published an extensive and growing list of titles which explore these processes and changes from a variety of perspectives.

Capitalism In The Age of Globalization:
The Management of Contemporary Society
Samir Amin

Women, Population and Global Crisis: A Political-Economic Analysis
Asoka Bandarage

The New Imperialism: Crisis and Contradictions in North–South Relations
Robert Biel

Cooling Down Hot Money: How to Regulate Financial Markets
Walden Bello, Nicola Bullard, Kamal Malhotra (eds)

The Globalisation of Poverty: Impacts of IMF and World Bank Reforms
Michel Chossudovsky

Impasses of Market Society
Christian Comeliau

Intellectual Property Rights, the WTO and Developing Countries:
The TRIPS Agreement and Policy Options
Carlos M Correa

Capital Accumulation and Women's Labour in Asian Economies
Peter Custers

An Introduction To The WTO Agreements
Bhagirath Lal Das

The WTO Agreements:
Deficiencies, Imbalances and Required Changes
Bhagirath Lal Das

The World Trade Organization:
A Guide to the New Framework for International Trade
Bhagirath Lal Das

Structural Adjustment, Global Trade and the New
Political Economy of Development
Diplab Dasgupta

The Limits of Capitalism:
An Approach to a Globalization Without Neoliberalism
Wim Dierckxsens

The Free Trade Adventure:
The WTO, the Uruguay Round and Globalism: A Critique
Graham Dunkley

The Age of Transition:
Trajectory of the World-System, 1945–2025
Terence Hopkins and Immanuel Wallerstein et al.

Neo-Liberalism or Democracy?
Economic Strategy, Markets, and Alternatives for the 21st Century
Arthur MacEwan

The Global Trap:
Globalization and the Assault on Prosperity and Democracy
Hans-Peter Martin and Harald Schumann

Global Futures: Shaping Globalization
Jan Nederveen Pieterse (ed.)

Eco-Socialism or Eco-Capitalism?
A Critical Analysis of Humanity's Fundamental Choices
Saral Sarkar

The Trouble with Capitalism:
An Enquiry into the Causes of Global Economic Failure
Harry Shutt

The Globalisation of Finance:
A Citizen's Guide
Kavaljit Singh

Taming Global Financial Flows:
Challenges and Alternatives in the Era of Financial Globalisation
Kavaljit Singh

Naming the Enemy:
Anti-Corporate Social Movements Confront Globalization
Amory Starr

100 Ways of Seeing an Unequal World
Bob Sutcliffe

The False Dilemma:
Globalisation – Opportunity or Threat?
Oscar Ugarteche

The Next Crisis?
Foreign Direct and Equity Investment in Developing Countries
David Woodward

For full details of this list and Zed's other subject and general catalogues, please write to:
The Marketing Department, Zed Books, 7 Cynthia Street, London N1 9JF
or email Sales@zedbooks.demon.co.uk

Visit our website at: http://www.zedbooks.demon.co.uk